# I Am the CLAY

## Anna Gideon

WESTBOW
PRESS®
A DIVISION OF THOMAS NELSON
& ZONDERVAN

Scriptures taken from the Holy Bible, New International Version®, NIV®. Copyright © 1973, 1978, 1984, 2011 by Biblica, Inc.™ Used by permission of Zondervan. All rights reserved worldwide. www.zondervan.com The "NIV" and "New International Version" are trademarks registered in the United States Patent and Trademark Office by Biblica, Inc.™

WestBow Press books may be ordered through booksellers or by contacting:

WestBow Press
A Division of Thomas Nelson & Zondervan
1663 Liberty Drive
Bloomington, IN 47403
www.westbowpress.com
1 (866) 928-1240

Because of the dynamic nature of the Internet, any web addresses or links contained in this book may have changed since publication and may no longer be valid. The views expressed in this work are solely those of the author and do not necessarily reflect the views of the publisher, and the publisher hereby disclaims any responsibility for them.

Any people depicted in stock imagery provided by Getty Images are models, and such images are being used for illustrative purposes only. Certain stock imagery © Getty Images.

ISBN: 978-1-9736-4658-7 (sc)
ISBN: 978-1-9736-4657-0 (hc)
ISBN: 978-1-9736-4659-4 (e)

Library of Congress Control Number: 2018913881

Print information available on the last page.

WestBow Press rev. date: 03/27/2019

# Contents

To the weary parents who persevere

# Preface

*"Have Thine own way Lord, Have Thine own way, Thou
art the potter, I am the clay. Mold me and make me, after
thy will, While I am waiting, yielded and still."*

— "Have Thine Own Way,"
Adelaide A. Pollard (1907)

When I was a little girl, no older than four, as my family returned
home from church I started playing a hymn I had heard at the 10
o'clock service. My parents were preparing lunch in the kitchen as
I effortlessly played the melody to the old hymn "Glorious is Thy
Name" on my brother's plastic organ that sounded like a jet airliner
when you plugged it in.[1] It was hardly an instrument. He didn't
really play it. In fact, no one in my family played anything, and I
was barely four. But my parents were astounded when they heard it
and thought I was musically gifted. With all the love in their hearts,
they immediately put me in piano lessons as they scraped together
some money to buy a second-hand piano.

I don't think they ever understood that I was just in love with music.
It governed most all of my thoughts. I had tunes playing in my
head all the time. I couldn't escape them, nor did I want to. I just
seemed to understand music. That's how I would describe it, an
understanding. It made perfect sense to me and I lived for it.

I loved it all. For Christmas, I received records and albums and a blue, fold up, record player from my cousin Mike. I was crazy about The Carpenters at first, then it moved to Boston when I discovered rock, but church hymns were still amongst my favorites of all.

I know now that these hymns somehow became a part of me. No one could possibly know how deep the roots of these four-part hymns are burrowed deep down in my soul. But as I grew older and grew to love the Lord and understand, the words became just as meaningful. These songs were like the most beautiful prayers set to music. There cannot possibly be any more beautiful or profound lyrics.

The very hymn, "Have Thine Own Way" is the one that felt the most special to my heart when I was a girl. Our music minister at church obviously felt the same way as it was the one that was played over and over during the invitation time. I must admit, I could never hear this one without feeling invited. It was like the Lord was calling me to do something. But what was it? Even many years after I invited Jesus into my heart, I never stopped feeling a call when I heard this song.

Many years later It would be the tune I heard as I was changing three diapers at once, rocking, loving, feeding, cooking, cleaning, and lying awake, having given up on sleep. I heard it all the time after my baby girl died and when my little son was diagnosed with autism. I most certainly heard it pervasively through the aftermath when I cried out in fear, sadness, and anger. Music is my language, and the Lord loves me enough to know that about me.

This song reminded me of the divine invitation to be the clay in the Almighty's hands—to surrender and let Him do His mighty handy work. He knew that I would have troubles, fears, and crises of faith.

He knew that I would need the words to this hymn in all of their meaning to overcome some of life's hardest knocks. He knew how significant they would be. He also knew I would need to know the depths of His perfect love for me.

As I persevered through some very difficult times, I would eventually be able to see God's fingerprints all over my life. I know He was involved, constantly intervening on my behalf and refining my character. The writing of this book was put on my heart many years ago, and It is my most sincere intent that the meaning of this great old hymn, "Have Thine Own Way" be lovingly and thoughtfully shared through my life experiences and in doing so, give to God the greatest glory.

# Acknowledgements

My most sincere thanks to the people who have stood by me through the most difficult times: My mother and father, my mother-in law and father-in law, and most of all—my wonderful husband whose love and support continue to sustain me. I would also like to thank Jamie, Lisbeth, and Drew. You are, in every way, the best kids in the world. You give me hope, strength, and purpose.

Thank-you Lisa and Cindy for your loving support and help. I treasure your input and your friendship.

Thank-you Cheryl and Connie for helping me with the huge task of editing.

I would also like to acknowledge: Tristan, Alexa, Seth, and Christian. Your kindness does not go unnoticed. You guys are a big part of this story and the best friends anyone could ever have!

Lastly, I would like to express appreciation for the wonderful staff at Westbow Press for their patience and professionalism.

# Introduction

It is true that everybody has a sad story. Well this is mine. It is a story mostly about loss and the stages of grief we navigate trying to make sense of it all. It is a story about a tragic stillbirth, a little boy locked in the lonely world of autism, a love crazed momma, and a sweet little family trying their best to cope with it all. But my story doesn't remain sad. The good news is that God is faithful and will restore the grieving heart, the anxious heart, the sad, and even the mad heart. He is a great healer of all things. We just have to put on the divine lenses of faith to see the miracles in our midst.

Struggles with parenting, education, behavior, and sibling relations are paramount to parents of special needs children. These are the battles day after day and year after year that wear us down. My prayer is that my story and experiences speak to them.

Truly there is nothing spectacular about me. I have no qualifications to write a book on autism or faith. I am not a biblical scholar, a doctor in behavioral science, or even a credentialed educator. I am not writing because I have accomplished some great feat or because I have morphed into some greater being who's enlightened and grasps life a little better than everyone else. In fact, I know myself as the world's "most forgiven sinner." I am pretty much despicable and certainly never worthy of the kind of love and grace that our Lord has bestowed on me. However, this love and grace is life changing. And it is in this heartfelt spirit that God has called me to share my story, my experiences, some great interventions, and insight that I gained along the way in regards to the autism epidemic. Without a doubt, there's a lot of good stuff to share.

This is a chronicle through the formative years of a child with autism. It is a testament to the good that the Almighty can make out of utter chaos, and how He is the ultimate remedy to despair, hopelessness, sadness, and anger. This is my story. This is Jamie's story. It is Amelia's, Beau's, Lisbeth's, and Drew's story. It is a story of powerful redemption. But much more significant, it is the story of God's endearing love for me, His provision, His compassion, His faithfulness, and the fact that assuredly, He loves you no less than me.

Isaiah 64:8 reads, "Yet you, Lord, are our Father. We are the clay, you are the potter; we are all the work of Your hand."

I know that He molds me and makes me exactly what He wants according to His purposes; and it is so good. I am beyond thankful that He continues to teach me, refining my character every step of the way. I am overwhelmed and elated by such goodness and grace, and I am so grateful and humbled to be "the clay"- His clay.

# Prayer

Let it not be my will but Thy will that is done in the writing of this book. Let every word ring through Your goodness, faithfulness, and divine compassion. Dear Heavenly Father, let every heart be touched and transformed by Your amazing love and mercy. I pray that Your message is delivered exactly as You desire it to be, under Your righteous direction and province. Let me show Your love for humankind through my deepest troubles, disappointments and brokenness. Let my imperfections show Your perfect strength and glory.

I want every discouraged parent of an autistic child to know Your unique design and plan for their child — that they would come to trust Your plan. For Your plan has the perfect peace they desire. I pray that they understand that our expectations for our precious children pale so far in comparison to what You have already designed. Please restore their hope and faith in You that they may become obedient in order to receive Your many blessings.

I pray for the brokenhearted who have lost a child through any circumstances, stillbirth or other tragic means. I ask You, Father, to comfort them and hold them in Your loving arms as You are *Abba*. May they come to receive so much love and healing from You that they are able to move on, live, and love again.

I pray for those who have been deeply wounded by this world so wrapped in Satan's lies. I pray deliverance for those bound by anger, resentment, and guilt. I ask that the rotten root of bitterness that strangles them be destroyed. Let the peace that surpasses all understanding reign in their hearts forever as they come to know and trust You.

Let us all come together in remarkable faith and proclaim Your mighty name. Help us to understand that true happiness and contentment come only through loving and serving You Father, the Living God.

Lord, I pray that this book honors You and praises Your holy name with every word. I beg You to mold us and make us according to Your precious will. Help us to yield to Your ways and wait on You with faith that can move mountains so that we may live every day to glorify Your name. This I pray through Jesus Christ, my Lord and Savior.

## Chapter One
# Our Story

*"And He walks with me and He talks with me and He tells me I am His own, And the Joy we share as we tarry there, none other has ever known."*

— *"In the Garden," Charles A. Miles (1913)*

Beau and I met on New Year's Eve in our home town in southern Louisiana in the year 1997. I was working as a registered nurse in a cardiac intensive care unit. I truly loved nursing. I loved every minute of holding tender, feeble old hands, ministering to the broken spirits of the sick and doing my best to restore dignity to the dying. It was my ministry. As I had lost my way through college and meandered through the secular world with my faith on the back-burner, my career as a nurse I feel, saved me. It gave me an identity and more purpose in my life than I had ever experienced. However, the job was like running a marathon every day.

After several years, I had to rethink my future. Although I loved my job, loved my fellow co-workers and my patients, I became restless, experiencing a bit of burn-out and boredom. I craved a new adventure in my life. The truth is I could never imagine myself falling in love and getting married. I was just too eccentric and free-spirited, so I went back to school full time in engineering. I attended classes during the week and worked all weekend. I absolutely loved my classes and found the challenge refreshing. (Though this sounds so heroic and ambitious, I only lasted a semester. It was all Beau's fault.)

Beau was working as a petroleum engineer at the time, and this gave us quite a conversation piece when we met. It all started with one fabulous date that led to him tutoring me in calculus. He was absolutely brilliant, unpretentious, hilarious, and completely immature when he wanted to be. We came to discover that we had so much in common.

We both came from loving Christian families, had attended the same church through childhood, and had grown up about a mile apart from each other, though we were barely acquainted. I was enamored with his brilliance and his heart, and much to my surprise, I fell deeply in love. I was very happy being single and loved my life, but he changed everything. The one thing that really cinched our relationship was that we both loved the Lord and were unashamed about our faith in Jesus.

We were married ten months later, the following November. My new adventure had replaced my old one. I decided to abandon school due to the cost and the stress, and I moved into emergency room nursing, which was new, challenging, and exciting.

Married life was wonderful, and we were both blissfully happy for a while, until we were hit by a storm. After only a few months of marriage, I had an early miscarriage. Although we were brokenhearted, miscarriages are fairly common and this would not have been highly unusual—except for the fact that during the ultrasound, the doctor noticed I had an abnormally shaped uterus. This doctor explained that I might have trouble maintaining a pregnancy due to this abnormality. I was twenty-eight when Beau and I married; and due to the fact that we were both excited about having a family, I was pretty concerned about this. After some research, I decided to consult a fertility specialist in New Orleans to confirm any problem.

I was privileged to meet a wonderful doctor there who quickly became a close friend of ours. He revealed that I had a vast uterine septum that would probably continue to restrict blood flow to potential embryos attempting to implant in the uterine wall. He predicted that maintaining a pregnancy would be difficult and that my rate of miscarriage would be very high. Although he did not push for the procedure, he did mention that he could surgically remove the septum, greatly increasing my chances of a healthy pregnancy. There was, however, also the risk that scar tissue resulting from the surgery could also complicate implantation. In any case, we opted for the surgery. My mother and mother-in-law were very supportive and traveled with me to the appointments, which were about a two-hour drive from our home.

A week before the scheduled surgery, I had to call the doctor and explain that I had a positive pregnancy test. We were anticipating surgery, and I was embarrassed. I couldn't imagine how we could have possibly miscalculated the timing. He, in very professional terms, explained how it happened. He sounded so relaxed and optimistic. I was a basket case and felt like a complete idiot. I was sobbing, worried I might have to endure another miscarriage. He kindly reassured me that this pregnancy might just survive. He encouraged me to come in that week so he could see what was going on. Our mothers and I took off to New Orleans again, not realizing how many times in the future we would make this trip.

During the ultrasound, the doctor conducted blood flow studies that revealed that when I was laying down, blood flow to the area of implantation was adequate, but when standing up, it was greatly compromised. His prescription? "Stay on bed rest for three months." He also put me on natural progesterone. It was quite a hard pill to swallow. I had to take a leave of absence from work and lay in the bed all day, only getting up to bathe and potty. It might sound marvelous to some, but it was very tough and lonely. I was by myself all day and completely unproductive. There is only so much T.V. and reading one can stand. My loved ones constantly reminded me that I did have a job nurturing my baby to full term. Truthfully, I was quite skeptical until morning sickness hit. I became insanely sick but thankful for every minute of it. At this time, I started to believe that our baby might survive. I thanked God continually and prayed day and night.

It was as though a miracle occurred when I made it through the first trimester with a healthy baby. We continued driving to New Orleans every two weeks for an ultrasound, and it was like Christmas morning every time I heard a heartbeat and saw movement on the screen. How amazing and rewarding it was to see our baby grow step by step every two weeks! This was one of the happiest periods of my life.

At about four months along I was able to continue on with a high-risk ob-gyn in Lafayette, another incredible doctor that greatly ministered to me and my whole family. At sixteen weeks, he elected to do a cervical cerclage procedure. (A cerclage entails stitching the cervix which helps prolong untimely preterm labor.) The odds were stacked against me that my cervix was strong enough to hold a pregnancy due to my uterine abnormality. This went smoothly and we were now getting excited. At twenty weeks, we found out we were having a precious baby girl.

Life was great. I was off of bed rest now, feeling wonderful, and we had just bought our first home. Beau was working hard helping to launch this new oil field service company, and our parents were helping us as we painted and remodeled. My doctor followed me closely with ultrasounds every two weeks, and the baby was developing perfectly. Genetic testing came back in the normal range, and normal growth patterns were observed.

Christmastime arrived and we were settled in our new house. Our baby's room was completed and absolutely adorable. I had just started buying baby stuff as I entered my third trimester. It was a magical Christmas full of wonder, excitement, and hope. The day after was not.

On December 26, 1999, I woke up a little spooked. In all the excitement of the holiday, I couldn't remember the last time I had felt the baby move. I really couldn't recall any movement at all on Christmas day. I did several things to elicit movement that morning, but I felt nothing. I called my doctor and was told to come in. I was really not that worried and headed over. Convincing myself that I was overreacting, I sat in the waiting room nonchalantly applying mascara.

Of course, the first thing they did was check the baby with the ultrasound. I had come to know the ultrasound tech pretty well and can still remember the look on her face after a few minutes. It was a look of horror. My heart started racing and I asked, "Is she moving?" She jumped up and said, "I need to get the doctor." He returned instantaneously, took a look, and gently gave me the bad news. It was surreal. It was unimaginable. I felt as though I was in the middle of a nightmare. The room was spinning and all of my senses smothered me. I could hear the buzzing of the florescent lights. My skin was burning and my body felt weak. My baby was dead. How could this be? I was truly in shock. I saw every precious moment I had with the promise of this beloved child flash right before my eyes. It was over just like that.

All I could think about was Beau. He was the only one I wanted to see or be with. I needed him. I wanted the only person who could truly understand this loss. It felt like he was there in five minutes, but I know it took him at least thirty. In the time I waited for him, I prayed to God to send me help. I did not think I could handle the loss. Frightened to death and in a state of shock, I kept praying, "God please help me. Please send me help. I can't do this alone." I begged him to come down from heaven and console me because it was just too much. I cried and prayed like never before. And then my help arrived. He was beautiful, about six feet tall, and wearing greasy red coveralls. Beau had arrived, and at that point I felt like I might live through this. He comforted me like no other.

I was immediately admitted to the hospital in preparation for an induction of labor. It was so incredibly sad. I was wheeled into one the happiest places on earth—the labor and delivery ward. Unlike all of the happy mommies there, my experience was one of great pain, suffering, and sorrow.

I had a "no visitors" sign on my door. I was unable to speak or think and certainly could not tolerate company. I mean, what was there to "visit" about? It took two days to deliver.

When the time came I was scared to death. Anxiety flooded over me as I had no idea what to expect. I did not know what she would look like and could never be prepared to hold my dead baby in my arms. I had no control over my emotions and did not know how I would react. I wasn't so sure I wouldn't die from the shock. A very sweet friend of mine happened to be my labor nurse. She was compassionate and gentle. When I cried to her about my fear of delivering the baby she simply said, "I know you are scared but I'll be here with you Anna." It was amazing how much that comforted me.

Our baby's name was Amelia. When she was delivered, she was absolutely beautiful. She looked so perfect and alive that I expected her to start breathing. I was grateful to have the opportunity to see and hold her for as long as I wanted, and to this day, I wish I had taken pictures. I was offered pictures, but in my grief, I just could not imagine "capturing the moment." It was my life's greatest tragedy. I felt like a picture would be a cruel reminder. I was wrong. I wish I had a picture of my sweet angel that awaits me in heaven.

There was never an answer to the cause of death. The doctor suspected a cord accident. The umbilical cord was unusually long and quite wrapped at delivery. I opted out of an autopsy. I couldn't fathom letting anyone cut my beautiful baby open.

We had a sweet and tender funeral for her. Our beloved family pastor conducted the ceremony and it was so very special. Our family was extraordinarily generous and supportive. They took over and carried us through. Beau and I were so grateful.

The grief over the next few months was incapacitating. In the early weeks, I would wake up forgetting that we had lost the baby. I would touch my flat belly and have to relive the nightmare over and over again. I woke up crying and went to bed crying. I slept with the blanket they swaddled her in every night. I am ashamed to say that I couldn't really stand to be around people, with the exception of Beau. I didn't want well-meaning people to distract me from the fact that the most horrible tragedy of my life up to that point had just occurred. I tried to venture out to the grocery store and such, but without fail, I was surrounded by pregnant bellies. I was convinced they were following me. I was constantly reminded of my loss as my sister-in-law, my cousin, Beau's cousin, and both of our best friends were all expecting around the same time as we were. Once so happy to be sharing in this joyous season with family and friends, I was heartbroken to be around them. I also felt guilty for feeling this way.

I was simply a mess. I was trying desperately to work through my grief so that I could return to work and to life. I prayed continuously to the Lord as I cried. I prayed for comfort, solace, and acceptance. I was never angry with God though. I knew in my heart He loved me. I could feel it like never before. I knew somewhere deep, very deep, that Amelia was always intended to be His, not mine. Though I was not angry, I had many doubts. I continued to question, "Why?" I could not understand why this happened. I remember crying to my best friend, "I don't understand. I prayed for her every day and every night. I prayed for her...." I was questioning the purpose of prayer and why we should even bother. I will never forget her profound answer.

She said, "Anna, remember that God answers prayers in His time, not ours."

I would think about this for a long time to come.

The Lord is faithful and just, and He did comfort me. Though I had to go through this, He continually brought me peace and angels.

There were so many tender moments where people reached out to me. I look back now and see the people God sent to remind me of His deep endearing love.

Once shortly after the funeral, I was coaxed to get out of the house and ride with my dad to Shreveport. He had always been so jovial and fun. And though neither one of us are ever at a loss of words, the trip was quiet. As I stared out the window silently with tears streaming down my face, he reached in his pocket and handed me a handkerchief. He looked at me with more compassion than a thousand words could ever convey. I have never known my dad to carry a handkerchief. He was prepared. And just being with him, I could absorb all of the empathy he had to offer. I felt comforted. I have learned that we can show love sometimes just by about being there—prepared and available. My mother, mother-in-law, father-in-law, granddaddy, and my Aunt Bobbi were all angels as well not to be minimized.

When you go through a tragedy, it seems you get a great amount of comfort from those who have suffered the same. I gained comfort from my grandmother and Beau's granddaddy who both lost a child as well as many close friends and family members who had endured such great loss. The comfort came from seeing that they survived. They were able to go through this horrible pain and managed to live through it. The scary part was that they knew their children and had precious memories. My baby never took a breath, opened her eyes, or moved, and the pain I felt was so excruciating I did not think I would ever make it through. This was frightening. The love I had for this baby was so powerful, I wasn't sure I could live without her.

One day, a dear family friend who had also lost a precious child was comforting me and brought me to the understanding that God is a parent too. She led me to see that He too grieves. He grieves over us daily, and most certainly grieved when his precious Son was tortured and crucified on the cross. It was at this moment that I was able to internalize the empathy and the great compassion that the Lord has for all of us.

I developed a supernatural relationship with the Lord at this time of great grief and sorrow. He was my only comfort. He was my everything. I know that this intense period of grief fostered this very special relationship. I did not hear His voice, but I did feel His overwhelming presence. Sometimes I truly wanted to be at home so I could be alone with Him. I just wanted the comfort of my heavenly Father who knew everything about me and loved me anyway. I felt like He mourned with me. As I continually prayed for comfort, I received it. It was an ongoing process. My hope and strength during this time was solely found in Him. And then I had "the dream."

Never before had I noticed anything supernatural happen in my life. Of course, I had never been so immersed into prayer either. I was your ordinary average sinner, no saint. I had a heated temper; I could be cynical, sassy, and even cussed when necessary. I marched to the beat of my own drum and hated following rules. Although I was not a model Christian and was definitely lacking in the holiness department, I have always owned a pure heart full of passionate love for God and others and was blessed to have a very clear and meaningful spiritual dream.

It was an auditory one. The only visual I had was standing in our hall bathroom. It was a conversation. I was talking to God, and there was no mistake. The voice was the most beautiful, calm, soothing, loving voice I had ever heard. To this day, I cannot recall the sound of the voice, only how it made me feel. It completely comforted me until I was at perfect peace. I knew that God was speaking to me with abounding love. There was no judgment or reprimand of any kind as I would have expected, just love. As my body began receiving what felt like healing, I vividly remember saying, "Thank-you Father."

He kindly replied, "I am God, but I am not the Father."

It was though I really didn't get it because I kept making the same mistake. I knew He was God, so I showered Him with praise again many times saying, "Thank-you Father."

Again, as before, He gently corrected me completely unprovoked and replied, "I am God, but I am not the Father."

It seemed important that I understand this distinction. His was the sweetest voice I had ever heard. He reassured me that everything was fine and how much He loved me. The voice was life-changing, and the conversation was so loving and convincing. I only remember one other specific thing He said. He intended to show me something— a vision that would greatly comfort me, but I would not remember it when I woke up. This is what I can recall from the dream. It was the most wonderful experience of my life, and I woke up changed.

The dream stayed with me, and I stewed on it for a while. This was significant. The Creator of the universe contacted me, and there was no mistake. I knew that God in some form had spoken to me, but I was bewildered and didn't know if I should tell anyone. I thought for sure, at that point, if I divulged this, my family would be seriously concerned about my mental health.

I simply could not get the whole experience out of my mind, so I phoned my brother Andy. He is one of the wisest people I know.

He also has a very special and sincere relationship with God. I have come to know him as a great philosopher of the faith. He seemed to be able to interpret it all. First of all, he believed me. Then he listened as I explained the nature of the voice. It became clear once I described the voice as counseling me.

He said, "Anna, I believe it was the Holy Spirit."

It made perfect sense. I was counseled and comforted. After he listened patiently, he also said he believed the vision I was shown might be our future children God had plans to bless us with. I knew in my heart he was right. I understood and felt overwhelmingly blessed.

The dream was definitely a turning point in my recovery. I also received great comfort from the scriptures explained in a book called "I'll Hold You in Heaven" by Jack Hayford.[1] The very scripture contained in 2 Samuel 12:23 was the only relief, the only hope I could sustain through this grief.[2] The author describes King David's infant son's death and the intense sorrow he endured. The words the King spoke, "I will go to him, but he will not return to me" revived my soul. I would see my baby daughter again. As a believer I would see her in heaven. She was not gone forever. She was waiting for me and we would one day reunite. I could finally live, assured of that.

I was eventually able to return to work six weeks later. I returned to my old job in the CICU. The stress level was much lower and predictable. I yearned to be around old friends. They were full of compassion and helped me transition back into normal life. I will never forget the special people God sent to help me along the way.

By the end of March, Beau and I were surviving and began to focus on having another baby, something I could have never fathomed before having the dream. It became the desire of my heart to have another baby. I didn't feel guilty, for no baby could replace Amelia. She was God's now. And though I still cried for her daily, my heart was able to move forward.

In time, I became a little obsessed with fertility, most likely from the fear of never being able to have a baby. For months, it was all I could think or talk about. Then one day I realized how much Beau loved me and how incredibly patient he had been with me through the whole ordeal. I then decided that this was not the right way to go about life. I needed to have faith and live with peace instead of angst. Fortunately, God answered my prayer a couple of months after my "baby crazy phase," and it happened.

Finally, we were expecting again. I never even considered the fact that I would miscarry. I was still indeed high risk, but I knew this baby was an answer to prayer. God intended for this baby to be ours, and I was never anxious. Though I was overjoyed, I was definitely still mourning the loss of our Amelia. Everything about the pregnancy reminded me of her, and I still cried for her every single day. I would literally carve out time in the evening to sit and cry. It was still bottled up; and grief never dissipates on its own. I was still working through it.

Upon examination of my first ultrasound, my doctor noted that the uterine septum that I once had was undetected. There was some speculation but no explanation. This can be said: I would never again experience a miscarriage.

I was quite relieved several months later when we found out we were expecting a boy. I needed to internalize that this was a totally different pregnancy with a totally different little soul onboard. We decided to name him James Ellison and did so with full confidence.

We thought the name strong and presidential. I felt so proud of my baby. I knew he would be someone very special, and I couldn't wait to hold him in my arms.

I was followed closely during the pregnancy. My doctor, who had literally cried with us when Amelia died, decided to induce labor as soon as the baby's lungs were developed. But it wasn't as easy as we thought. On the day I was admitted to the hospital for induction, I was sent home because he had, for the first time in the pregnancy, turned breech. I couldn't believe it. Not once in eight and a half months had he been in breech position. I was begging to stay as they wheeled me down to the front door. I so wanted my baby. I went home and prayed knowing for certain that he would turn.

The next morning, I call my doctor and said confidently, "I'm going back to the hospital now. He's head first." He was skeptical and said that he doubted that could have happened. He told me I had better come in to the office first to be checked. I was right. No one in the office could believe that the baby, being over seven pounds, had turned back like that. I had to admit that we had some serious intervention—our family friend Ms. Carol, the fiercest prayer warrior I know, praying for the baby to turn.

The induction of labor was not good. My epidural failed miserably all five times, and the progression of labor halted when I was seven centimeters dilated. I stayed at seven centimeters for many hours. I was on heavy doses of oxytocin, a hormone used to induce labor that produced nothing except excruciating pain. In fact, I was on such a heavy dose that they had to check my uterus to make sure it would not rupture. I would later scratch my head about these circumstances.

I finally grabbed my dear doctor by his white collar and pulled him close as I demanded, "Take me to the O.R. now!"

He did. There was only one problem I forgot about as they wheeled me into the O.R. for a long-awaited c-section—my epidural was not working.

That evening our James Ellison was finally born. He was healthy, beautiful, and very much alive. The joy we all felt is impossible to explain. The waiting room was full of family and friends, even some who drove from out of town. It was the happiest event of my life. We felt like we were living a miracle.

I remember waking in the middle of the night grabbing my IV pole, walking down to the nursery and pleading for him. I slept with him every night. "Jamie," as we decided to call him, had so many visitors. This was such a happy time. Our parents were overjoyed as well and just as lovesick as we were over our little fellow. These were precious memories that I would never forget.

When we were finally able to bring him home, we soon found out that he had colic. It seemed to get worse at night. In fact, he cried most every night for hours. I was happy to rock him and soothe him all night long, but many times I could not calm him down. This greatly upset me as I could barely stand to hear him cry. After a couple of months with no sleep, I was feeling weary, and worse— I felt like I couldn't comfort him. I wondered if he had even bonded with me. But there were good days, and I surely treasured them.

Around six months, he had a short stage where he was playful and looked happy at times. We enjoyed our baby and had so much fun playing with him. Though he was growing out of the colic stage, he was still very temperamental. At times, he seemed like a typical six-month-old. He was certainly meeting all of the milestones. Some days he would interact perfectly. But there were days I rarely saw him smile, and I noticed that he didn't really respond to me. It was though I wasn't there. He didn't hold up his arms for me to pick him up or act attached to me at all. Of course, I was the only one who saw this. Everyone else was quick to say I was being silly. I was really worried about him. Actually, I thought it was me. Perhaps I just wasn't good at being his mother. Insecurities flooded over me constantly. I was already nervous about keeping him alive. I wanted so desperately to give him the world and shower him with more love than any baby had ever known. I could not figure out what I was doing wrong.

I had learned to read his cues pretty well after a few months and would bring him in a dark, quiet, room when he became upset. I would pat him and whisper to calm him down. Also, I could not bring him anywhere if he was the least bit tired or hungry. I planned outings very carefully. I developed a pretty stringent schedule for him. It felt a little ridiculous, but I knew it was necessary. I worried quite a bit and felt internally that something was not quite right. No one else saw anything alarming. I had a great deal of anxiety after he was born, and that's mostly what others could see.

## Living the Dream

Big changes came for our family when Beau was transferred to Houston, Texas. Jamie was about ten months old. We were excited for a new adventure. Jamie was already walking and seemed to be interacting more. He would play, laugh, and snuggle. He actually appeared happy, and I was so relieved. This was a wonderful time. I was also pregnant again with our second child, and we were overjoyed. It felt like a pure blessing. Though I was six months pregnant with a ten-month-old and making a major move, I was ok because I felt that Jamie was developing normally. It seemed that my well-being was linked to his somehow.

I AM THE CLAY

Though we were just a four-hour car drive from family, Jamie and I were alone during the day and spent a lot of time together. I had given up working at this point and was looking forward to spending this precious time with my babies. I read to him constantly. We did puzzles and even started on picture flash cards. I taught him nursery rhymes, the parts of the face and body, the entire alphabet, and numbers to twenty. He was obviously very bright and never failed to hit the appropriate milestones. Also, he was starting to respond to my affections which delighted my soul. I did, however, see him as very demanding and quite high maintenance, but I kept him on a tight schedule and this worked beautifully. I never let him get too tired, too hungry, or uncomfortable; to allow these meant huge melt-downs. These inconsolable tantrums really made me a nervous wreck, so I used much more than an ounce of prevention to avoid them. Ventures out and about were difficult. So apart from wagon rides up the street and occasions to the park, we stayed home.

Around his first birthday, something in Jamie changed. He started demonstrating some peculiar behaviors that directly corresponded with the timing of his MMR vaccination. Looking back, I remember immediately following this vaccination, he had a horrible intestinal virus. For three weeks he had white, frothy, intensely foul-smelling poops. His diapers would become saturated several times a day and would leak all over. I gave him several baths a day for a while. Of course, I brought him to the doctor who pretty much dismissed it. I even took him to the E.R. once for fear he would dehydrate. He was lethargic and starting to look really skinny because he was unable to keep any food or milk down without vomiting.

After about three weeks the virus subsided, but behavioral changes followed. Sadly, he was my first born, and I didn't have the experience under my belt to recognize them.

My mother had given him a CD at birth of the most beautiful lullabies known to man. He listened to them every night, and the music soothed him greatly. His room had French doors with glass panes, and he would methodically place the square CD case to fit in all the corners of the panes he could reach. This would not have been so odd if he weren't fascinated with it for long periods of time with no regard for anything or anyone else.

He seemed uninterested in toys now. Instead, he enjoyed running back and forth waving a belt we had previously tied to a pull toy. He would mutter to himself and squeal as if he were on a rollercoaster, scampering along the same exact path. My mother-in-law, who faithfully visited every two weeks, remarked about the strange behavior once or twice as did my mother when she came. I rationalized it all. I had explanations for everything, and they were good: He was highly intelligent. He was a deep thinker, or perhaps he was just creative. I rationalized everything he did and decided to relax for once and quit worrying so much about my baby. I was going to accept him, appreciate his uniqueness, and enjoy this precious time we had together.

I tried very hard to keep my paranoid concerns in check. But there was a sadness inside me. I knew. I adored him from head to toe and smothered him with love and attention. He was my heart and soul; but I knew he was not a typical child. I did pray casually about Jamie, but I felt as though God gave him to me as a precious gift and it was up to me to help him and figure it all out. I was not immersed in prayer at this time, and my faith was pretty weak. I relied on only myself to get things done, feeling solely responsible for his well-being and development.

I cannot describe how sad and anxious I became inside. This was the child I pleaded with God for. On my knees day and night, I prayed and begged for him. And now my precious child graciously granted to me was miserable most of the time, and I couldn't soothe him. I felt relentless guilt as I was becoming miserable too. I didn't feel like we ever bonded. I didn't even feel like he liked me. There weren't smiles, tickles, cuddles or the memorable tender moments I had envisioned. I felt like a complete failure most of the time but never stopped trying to meet his needs. There was no way that I would ever stop trying to connect with him and help him to find joy.

Our darling Lisbeth was born three months after our move to Houston. As the labor and delivery ward was full, I had to share a semi-private room and could not have anyone stay with me. After my second c-section, I was left alone with my fears about Jamie. I remember feeling so isolated in my worry and sadness.

As soon as I could walk after the delivery, I went to the nursery and got my baby girl. It felt like the instant I held her in my arms, my loneliness subsided. From the minute she was born, she was alert, attentive, and was immediately comforted by my affection. I never knew how much love a heart could hold. She certainly filled mine. She was beautiful like a china doll with ruby red lips, big bright eyes, and the sweetest little face. She stayed right with me, and we held on to each other for dear life. She was delicate, needy, and always responsive to my love. The Lord richly blessed me that day with a very special daughter who was able to turn my fear and sadness into joy. Lisbeth's birth truly gave me a renewed sense of hope.

I was elated to bring Lisbeth home. She too, was surrounded by family that welcomed her with all the love in the world. When I walked in the door with her, to my surprise, Jamie made a beeline running full force to greet and hug me. His arms were outstretched, and he was grinning from ear to ear. My heart was overjoyed as I bent down to grab him and smother him with kisses. As I did, my incision split open and hemorrhaged a bit. We bandaged it up the best we could. I did not care, worry, or wonder. I was on top of the world. He had never greeted me like that before.

My mother and mother-in-law stayed about two weeks to help out. They were truly wonderful and so very appreciated. But it seemed the minute they left, Jamie and I both developed pink-eye, my c-section incision got badly infected from the incident, and worst of all, I developed a horrendous kidney stone. It was a rough time. Thankfully, we all survived, and life with two babies began.

I was starting to feel normalcy around the house with little Lisbeth added to the brood. I could no longer focus and dwell on Jamie and his development. I can't say it wasn't tough having two little ones fifteen months apart; it really was. It was much more difficult and demanding than I could have ever imagined. Some days were pretty lonely because I was without family or friends. I was very grateful for my mother-in-law, Nana, who faithfully visited. We enjoyed her company tremendously.

During this time, both children had chronic ear infections. Jamie had been on many rounds of antibiotics before Lisbeth was born. The pediatric group I used had the best reputation in the area, however, the doctor continued to prescribe stronger and stronger antibiotics each time. I did, many times, ask him if pressure equalizing tubes (P.E. tubes) might be more appropriate rather than continuing to medicate my child. His answer was no. He maintained that tubes did not prevent ear infections. He basically said that if we opted for surgery, Jamie would still have infections and continue to need antibiotics regardless. I blindly trusted this doctor and did not question him. Beau's father, a retired general practitioner, did question the overuse of the antibiotics, suggesting tubes were a better solution. I know now that he was right. This antibiotic abuse destroyed the normal flora in his gut leading to digestive troubles and was a prelude for problems to come.

Lisbeth's ear infections were actually much worse than Jamie's. She had chronic bilateral ear infections and suffered greatly. As fluid remained on her ears, antibiotics did her no good. Poor little Lisbeth suffered for many months. I hysterically sobbed when she got those nasty, painful antibiotic shots in her tiny little legs. It hurt my soul. She also suffered with tummy pain and gas much worse than Jamie ever did.

The babies seemed to be chronically sick, and their stomachs were always upset. I began to regret making the decision not to breastfeed my babies. I was overwhelmed with the idea at that time and decided that formula would be easier. I was certainly remorseful about the decision now. It seemed like there was no formula that would agree with little Lisbeth. She spit up all the time and was in constant discomfort. The pediatrician finally put her on a popular reflux medicine that helped some. Jamie also had never really done well with formula and continued to be fussy.

Neither baby slept well at night nor did they nap during the day. I could successfully put them to bed on a reasonable schedule, but there were several awakenings every night without fail. Jamie woke several times every single night, and Lisbeth often woke up with ear or stomach pain. Needless to say, I never got any rest. This long period of sleep deprivation would one day come to haunt me.

As my behavior was becoming a consequence of how little sleep I was getting, I finally began to get aggravated with the pediatrician and demanded that P.E. tubes be placed in both children. I had learned that countless rounds of antibiotics were detrimental to their tummies and immune systems. I had to fight him by arguing that the stagnate fluid needed to be drained and by showing him research where most ear infections are viral in nature. I finally won, got the much sought-after surgery that greatly helped my babies, and gained a "crazy mom" reputation all at the same time.

Days were in and out with Jamie. He seemed to respond to us more on some days than others, but he was progressing. At eighteen months he even passed the developmental screening test at the pediatrician's office (the CHAT test). Although I noticed he was behind with language as compared to other babies his age, he was beginning to have a few words and short phrases. In fact, by age two, he could count to twenty and recognize all of his ABC's and colors. He could also name most parts of the face and body and could recite some of his favorite books and nursery rhymes. However, he was a bit aloof socially and preferred to play alone.

He was such a sweet baby and appeared to emerge a little more as he approached two. He loved Lisbeth and seemed to interact with her a bit. I would put them both in the baby pool, and they would splash and squeal. Often, we would all play together in the backyard. I pulled them in the wagon to the park and swung them back to back on the baby swing. I will never forget the day we knelt across the living room as Lisbeth approached her first birthday and Jamie gleefully shouted, "Walk Lisbeth walk!" as she took her first steps. He was right there cheering her on with me. She was so adorable, and he was so excited for her. I believe, at this time, he was coming around.

During the time Lisbeth was born, we had a very sweet neighbor, Sharon, across the street. She knew I was interested in returning to work part-time. She needed a job and gladly offered to stay with the babies during the day at our house. I could not refuse because she was a very calm, cool, and loving person. She also had a little grandson Jamie's age that would accompany her. I thought it would be perfect for Jamie to have a role model for appropriate play, and perhaps more language would come out of it.

I landed a job in a local hospital ER. On my first day of work orientation, I returned home that afternoon from being gone all day, and strangely enough, Jamie would not acknowledge me. He treated me like I was invisible. He would not look at me nor come to me as I begged for a hug and a kiss. I picked him up, and he squirmed to get down as to get away from me. I had never before been separated from him that long, and I felt certain he would be overjoyed to see me. I can't explain how awkward and unusual it was. I was saddened and hurt but decided that he might be have been a bit disgruntled with me for leaving him all day. Still, I felt that this was an atypical response from a two-year-old.

I only worked about two shifts a week. It seemed like a great idea keep up my skills and contribute to the family income. I really enjoyed the job but found myself running red lights and speeding to get home at night because I missed my babies so very much. I only worked for a few months due to another complication— I discovered I was pregnant with number three.

Lisbeth was five months old, and Jamie was about nineteen months. I was completely shocked and overwhelmed. I continued working after the discovery but started seriously hemorrhaging around sixteen weeks. I assumed I had lost the baby. I was working when this happened and was privy to an exam and an ultrasound. Our baby was just fine. It was another precious little boy. The bleeding was benign and eventually resolved, but I resigned from my job because I felt I had my hands full.

To add more drama to the picture, we decided to move across town to minimize Beau's travel. Truly, moving across Houston is not really an inner city move but more like an out-of-state one. Luckily, Beau's father helped us physically move, and my mother helped us unpack. It was tough. We moved over an hour away. I absolutely dreaded moving away from Sharon.

Andrew Cooper Gideon, aka "Drew," was born on July 28th 2003. He was an angel. He was so happy and content. He rarely cried at all. He was grateful to be held, snuggled like a champ, and was also happy to be put down to play or sleep. He was an adorable little baby, and we all fell in love with him.

I will never forget my special Aunt Nellie who came and stayed with us, along with my mother, for three weeks to help me with the babies. She was so kind, fun, humorous, and extremely helpful. Before Drew was born I was petrified. I didn't know how I was going to manage after a third c-section. She came, not out of obligation, but because she wanted to help. She was delighted to help me with the babies, even waking at night with Drew for feedings. She was so kind to me —an angel sent by God. Some people you just never forget. She will be forever on my mind and in my heart.

On the dreadful day that Aunt Nellie left, real life began. Days were so hectic with three A.M. bottle feedings, diaper changes, meals, dishes and the laundry. It was like climbing a mountain each day, but I loved it and must admit that I did it well. I even cooked three meals a day. My babies were always fed, always clean, played with, and cuddled. I was still not getting more than three hours of sleep each night, but I was getting acclimated to it. (The daily pot of coffee I was consuming helped a great deal.) I truly enjoyed every minute of caring for them, playing with them and being a mommy. I had my hands full, but our home was never a stagnate environment.

There was always reading, games, finger painting, music, pretend play, and ventures outside. Though we were home all alone during the day, I assumed that all three babies were given adequate love, attention, and plenty of stimulation. I really tried. I never wanted any child to feel left out or minimized. But as hard as I tried, I could not make that happen.

Jamie was having monstrous meltdowns and tantrums. I never knew what would set him off; I just knew that he was in agony. He would bang his head as hard as he could on the floor and wail, "I bumped it." He would grab his hair, or mine, and pull as though his life depended on it. Sometimes he would take his fingernails and claw, mangling the flesh on his little face. No matter what I was doing, I had to immediately stop and pick him up to soothe and calm him. On many occasions, I was rocking Lisbeth or Drew to sleep and had no choice but to put them down to rescue Jamie. Once, I had Lisbeth in my lap reading her favorite book (she was so delighted to have my attention), and Jamie began one of his meltdowns. When I put her down, she started hurling books at me. She was frustrated. It happened a lot. I felt so helpless and wept as I picked Jamie up and saw the resentful, sad little baby on the ground who finally gave up and moved on to another toy.

These meltdowns, which he really always had, were getting worse. When I mentioned my concern to my family or my doctor, they pretty much just giggled and called it the "terrible twos." Our mothers continued to rant that we needed help. But the fact of the matter was that we did not have an extra salary to pay a nanny with, not even part-time. We were operating a family of five on one income. Also, I was certain that no one could keep up with the pace of our house. Surely, anyone working for ten dollars an hour would never stay. It was just too much work. I had tried a couple of ladies from time to time whom I hired to simply help out. No one ever came back.

In the meantime, I kept trying to problem-solve Jamie's meltdowns. I feared it was lack of socialization with peers his own age or the monotony of being at home every day. I laid awake each night thinking of what I could possibly do differently.

When Drew was about four months old, I started bringing the babies on outings but soon found out how difficult this would be all by myself as Jamie did not have the maturity of a typical three-year-old. Often times, he would melt down or worse —run off, which created constant panic.

I continued to take them out and about on occasion. I finally learned where we could go successfully. There was a small little park by our house that had enough to keep everyone busy and within a small safety zone. It was also shaded with big oak trees. I had come to realize that Jamie could not tolerate being in direct sunlight. There was also a wonderful playland at the mall that would keep them all happy and busy for a short period.

I often tried getting together with other mommies and their babies, but it was usually a disaster. When we would go to the bounce house places, Jamie would venture behind the structures and try to unplug everything. I was usually chasing him around as he would head for the door. Also, he would try to rip or destroy things or spit. His behavior was always a problem. I was always defeated and soon gave up socializing as I got tired of apologizing.

During these early years, the babies continued to stay sick with strep throat, sinus infections, and bronchitis. Drew was also having chronic ear infections and eventually earned his very own set of P.E.

tubes. It seemed like everyone was always stopped up, coughing, or running fever (including Beau and I). It was a very difficult time, and I was becoming more and more concerned about Jamie.

I felt his behaviors were beyond the scope of the "terrible twos." He was continuing to have frequent meltdowns with the head banging. I had tenaciously brought my concerns to the pediatrician who would chuckle and dismiss everything nonchalantly. I eventually had enough chuckling and had to put my hand on my hip. I insisted that he do a head C.T. on Jamie. I persisted that he must be having awful headaches. Something had to be hurting him. He grabbed at his little head all the time. I knew there was a problem, and enduring the scorn and criticism of many who thought I was ridiculous, Jamie got a C.T. of his head. It proved unremarkable with some evidence of sinusitis. I didn't feel ridiculous; I felt helpless. Though I was truly relieved it was not a tumor or such, I now knew there was more to the story. Perhaps it was something I was doing or failing to do hindering his development.

So I wondered: Is he getting enough rest? (He would never nap.) Is he feeling sad because he used to have all of my attention and now he must share me with two siblings? Had I just spoiled him rotten to his detriment? Did he need to be in preschool? Was he just unhappy? I was baffled, but not really. I continuously had autism on my mind. I had it on my mind from the time he was five months old and didn't appropriately respond to me. I had it on my mind for years as my brother mentioned the symptoms and verbalized concerns about one of his own children. It had been on my mind day and night. He had a language delay that my pediatrician would not acknowledge. He certainly had very limited socialization skills, and he had peculiar repetitive behavior. I also noticed that he played differently than other children.

Jamie was always a little odd when he played. He was ultimately obsessed with "Blues Clues." His favorite toy was a "Handy Dandy Notebook," a toy prop from the television program. He would run back and forth on the same path muttering gibberish shouting, "A clue!" And heaven forbid if he lost it. There was no remedy. He would terrorize the whole household upon losing the notebook or the crayon. I eventually visited every Walgreens in Northwest Houston and bought every "Handy Dandy Notebook" I could find.

Another favorite toy was a "Blues Clues House." It came with all the cool characters, but he would sit for periods turning it upside down opening and closing the door. In contrast, when Lisbeth played with it, she would decorate the house with the pieces and make the characters talk. Also, at this point, when I would sit down on the floor to read to them, he would get up and skip off. I tried putting him in my lap. Nothing worked. I could not make him sit still and listen.

It seemed like the symptoms became more noticeable after Drew was born. Fear paralyzed me every time I called his name and he would not turn to look as though he was in his own little world and far from me. He looked totally normal. In fact, he was extraordinarily beautiful with his shiny flaxen blonde hair and crystal blue eyes. But he did not respond like the other children. His odd mannerisms seemed to be apparent only to me, his emotional basket-case mother who analyzed his every utter or awkward movement. Every day I lived to prove to myself that he did not have autism, and every day I found another adequate reason to be hopeful. I did, however, face the possibility that if he was developing typically, that I could be suffering from some deep psychological issues. I remember praying for my own proven insanity.

My concerns, at this time, would waffle because he would always counter my fears with typical behaviors and milestones. And because he did have good days, I felt crazier than ever and assumed that all of this must be my fault. Family members and friends eased my concerns constantly. They saw no cause for concern. These periods of normalcy probably prevented him from getting an early diagnosis.

I thought structured socialization might help and eventually enrolled Jamie and Lisbeth in a wonderful little Lutheran preschool near our home. It had the best reputation in town, and we were lucky to have won a spot by lottery. Lisbeth was close to two years of age, and Jamie was three.

It took about a week for the teacher to call me in. As we conferenced with the director, she brought up concerns about his attention. As the class was involved in an activity, Jamie would aimlessly roam the room. He would not participate or respond. At lunchtime, he would grab everyone's food and run away with it. She verbalized concerns about his language delay and his delay in toilet training. (We had begun toilet training and it was going slow as he had very little language.) She also noticed that he didn't really play with the other children. She recommended that I get him evaluated by the school district. I have to admit, I was mortified as though I had no idea he had any delays. It was like it was all a fabrication of my imagination lest someone mention it out loud. She did; I was distraught, a tiny bit angry, and most of all overwhelmingly anxious.

Needless to say, I pulled him out of that school. I rationalized that the teacher was too strict and impersonal. I just wanted him home where he was understood and loved. After all, I figured they were too little to go to preschool. But my fears escalated as I continued searching for answers.

Jamie was cranky most of the time and was still having huge tantrums at home. I noticed he had many strange rashes that would come and go. I was also noticing that his ears would turn blood red after mealtimes. I began to speculate, "a happy baby is a healthy baby" so I brought him to an allergist who, after evaluating him, recommended allergy shots. He also mentioned food allergies as a possible culprit. He suggested we do a milk challenge where we would withhold all milk for a week and reintroduce it in large quantities on the eighth day to see if there were any noticeable consequences. I eventually did this, and the results were astonishing. I never expected there to be behavioral changes. During the week without milk, Jamie started talking more, there were no tantrums, he began to tinkle on the potty, and starting sleeping through the night for the first time. I never re-introduced the milk on the eighth day. I could not have been paid to.

I did finally make an appointment with the school district to get him evaluated. The lady who did the evaluation did not appear to have a compassionate or caring bone in her body. She was stuffy, impersonal, and appeared to take "professional" to a new level. He was three and a half. Of course, he didn't cooperate with someone like that. She called me a couple of days later and rightfully recommended the school district's special developmental preschool program for Jamie. I had predetermined that I didn't like this lady. I didn't want her help. I did not believe she had any feelings or concern for him, nor did she understand what he needed. I declined when she called to offer the program. I am ashamed to admit that I was a tad bit cynical on the phone. I was frustrated. She was supposed to tell me he was a brilliant little boy and that there was no problem. I had one foot in denial and the other in reality.

I had suspected for some time that Jamie was on the autism spectrum. I hadn't really slept in months. On the occasion that I had a few hours of peace, I would lie awake trying to make sense of it all. I tried to reason out all of the gaps in his development—all the peculiar behaviors. I would lie there for hours, sometimes my heart racing as I silently cried. I did pray. I prayed and begged God for direction, wisdom, and peace, but I received little solace through my torment because I honestly had very little faith. During these early years, I thought I was the one to fight the battle. I believed it was up to me to find the cause and the cure—that it was up to me, alone, to change his life. I was afraid, desperate, and overwhelmed.

Some days the fear was unbearable. The enemy of God had me so wrapped in despair and lies that I could hardly breathe. I started believing that I had obviously caused some terrible developmental disconnect in my child, and worse, that the fate of my other two children would be the same. I started to believe it was my fault.

I tried so hard to make it not true. I cuddled more, played more, and read more. I put on puppet shows, made tents, sculpted animals with playdough, worked puzzles with them, and sang and danced tirelessly. We drew with chalk, played games in the bathtub and I taught them to play hide-and go-seek. I even had a round laundry basket I would put them in to spin across the kitchen floor like and amusement park ride. I knew I could help Jamie along. I was absolutely convinced I could do it. He had such sad eyes. I never tired of trying to make him smile.

People were pretty uncompassionate during this time. Many said I was overwhelmed with three babies so close together, and some thought I was losing it. No one could see what I could see. There were many cutting comments, unfair accusations, and condescending attitudes. I was starting to build a wall of internal resentment that would later take years to break down. I felt like the people I loved and trusted the most in all the world were scoffing and turning their backs on me. There was plenty of chuckling, eye rolling, and criticism, but no one who could possibly understand what was really going on.

I remember vividly the night I approached Beau for the millionth time crying about my concern for Jamie. He said something I will never forget. He looked at me square in the eye and said, "Anna, we've all been talking about this and we think that Jamie is fine, but we think something may be going on with you." Knowing how fragile I was, I probably rested well that night for it must have relieved my branded soul to hear this. I wanted so desperately to hang on to my denial.

After many nights of wrestling with all of the junk in my head, I came to a couple of conclusions. I knew Jamie's language was delayed. (The pediatrician agreed but was not at all worried about it.) I also knew that his social development was lacking. He seemed to need a more structured environment that provided plenty of socialization with children his own age. But most of all, what he really needed was a healthy mother with all of her sanity.

The perfect answer became putting the three kids in daycare as I returned to work a couple days a week. I thought I might regain some perspective, and the children would learn some important social skills. It seemed like the perfect solution since there would be no nosy teacher constantly reminding me of Jamie's developmental delays. It was a tad bit absurd that I went back to work in order to put my children in daycare, but I was desperate for a plan.

I wish I could say that I loved my job and that Jamie, Lisbeth, and Drew were thriving, but I can't. I was miserable. I was working at one of Houston's larger hospitals in a tragically disorganized

E.R., and it was tough. I only worked two to three shifts a week, but they were twelve-hour shifts, and the babies literally mobbed me when I got home.

Beau had installed chain locks on the doors to the house when the children learned to unlock the doors and proceed to stroll around the neighborhood at will. When I arrived home after work, there would be three heads stacked one on top of the other peering at me through the three inches of the door crack. Drew was on bottom with his green Oscar shirt, Lisbeth was in the middle with her red Elmo shirt and Jamie on tiptoes with his blue Cookie Monster one. They were whining for me and would have busted through that door if they could have.

Most nights I would strip my clothes off in the garage and walk in with undergarments on for fear of what might have followed me home. It was heaven to walk in that door and have so much love waiting. I missed them terribly on those days, but I had started this arrangement and intended to see it through. I needed to see if the time away from me socializing with peers would help Jamie. I knew that Lisbeth and Drew were just fine, in fact, ahead of the game in every aspect. They only needed my love and attention. Jamie needed so much more.

During these months at daycare, no one ever mentioned that Jamie's behaviors were odd or that he struggled. I was only told that he was a bit aloof. This did not bother me too much for I knew it was true of him. I tried not to inquire about him. I just wanted to let things be without any preconceived ideas. I worked for about three months when I had to re-evaluate the situation.

We had met a precious girl named Hannah that worked at the daycare. She started babysitting on occasion when Beau and I wanted to get out of the house and go to dinner. She was very good with the kids, and I trusted her. On one occasion when she was babysitting, I asked her before she left if she thought Jamie was doing well. I shared some of my concerns about him. When I prompted her, she began to open up to us. She told us that the other workers would not ask him to participate in clean-up because they said he was "not all there." She said that he was always alone and never played with any of the other children. She said the staff also made fun of him because he was not yet fully potty- trained. She was really distraught by this, and I could tell it had been on her mind for a while. Once again, I was shocked and my whole body went numb. I was very thankful Hannah was honest with us.

The very next day I pulled all of the kids out of that daycare setting. I switched to weekends at work and was overjoyed to have them home with me again. Beau would take care of them on Saturday and Sunday. I was now over my head, and I knew it. It was time for some serious intervention.

Now at three and a half, Jamie still just had short phrases like "Go night night," "Take a bath," and "Wanna eat." Having Lisbeth, who was now two and completely potty-trained, allowed me to see the developmental delay. She was having complete, quite mature, conversations with me. His language was always functional. It was always about what he needed. He did not really answer questions or talk back.

I began to see clearly that his language was delayed. And though I had brought this to the attention of my pediatrician time and time again, I hung my hat on this as the reason for all of the behaviors. I wondered if this was causing him to become isolated. I figured that the language delay alone could cause him to feel locked away from the world. After all, what connects us to each other is communication.

I had left the old pediatric group and was trying out a new one. I had so much faith that they would have all of the answers. I brought my concerns about Jamie's language delay to the doctor. She was very compassionate and listened. She examined him and began to assess his language. She asked him to say "cat," and he said it in his scratchy little voice. Then she asked him to repeat "dog," and he did. She continued with a few more words, and then looked at me and said she thought he was just fine. She concluded that boys were slower to talk than girls and that she expected his language to begin to progress soon. I expressed concern that he might have an autism spectrum disorder. She said that she very much doubted that. As much as I craved hearing this, I was still apprehensive and asked for a speech evaluation referral. She was happy to give it to me.

As I waited for the speech evaluation, I immersed myself in books about autism, mostly concerning biomedical interventions such as diet and nutritional supplements. I was impressed with what I saw from the milk challenge and was eager to learn more. There were about three books on the shelf. The year was 2004, and the world had not yet become acquainted with the American epidemic. I was binge reading everything I could get my hands on. I knew now I wasn't crazy. I was pretty convinced my son had an autism spectrum disorder. I did not feel any better realizing that I was sane after all.

I began to talk to everyone I met about Jamie. I would constantly tell his story and ask for advice. In my desperate networking attempts, I was given the name of a naturopath in Houston that was greatly improving the lives of many children on the autism spectrum. I immediately called and had Jamie's name added to his long waiting list. I started reading quite extensively about the biomedical interventions available now for autism. I would leave no stone unturned.

ANNA GIDEON

Our family visited often but still could not see the disconnect. He was sweet and affectionate and lively at times. But I was with him enough to know that he wasn't fully participating in life. I noticed that he started in a downward spiral after receiving the flu vaccination in the winter of 2004. He clearly took a turn for the worse, and family members were starting to notice the changes.

Our slightly odd but adorable little boy became even more isolated and sad. There was now a clearly defined change. He appeared so very unhappy and disengaged with the world. We noticed that he would clasp his hands over his ears in response to certain sounds and would not play, or even resemble anything that looked like play. Now, he would sit on the floor making "garage doors" with large rectangular books, lifting them up against the frame of a small table while pushing a car through. He did explain what he was doing, and it sounded pretty creative except for the fact that he did it over and over tirelessly. He would not allow anyone to participate either. He simply did not want to be disturbed. He would do "garage door" for an hour if we did not intervene. He would also play "garage door" with small flash cards, moving them up and down somehow. As with the repetitive behavior, was his repetitive language.

He would repeat catch phrases over and over again. At first, we thought it was cute, but I eventually became disturbed by how non-functional it was. I also wondered about his hearing. He often times would not turn around as I called his name. He rarely followed commands or answered back. Distraught by the unusual changes I was witnessing, I arranged an appointment with an E.N.T. in the area to have his hearing evaluated. I was now hanging onto the hope that all of his problems could be the result of a hearing deficit.

The time for the anticipated speech evaluation finally arrived. The report showed significant expressive and receptive language deficits. The young lady who evaluated him was very competent and felt inclined to tell me she believed he had P.D.D., or Pervasive Developmental Disorder. This fancy terminology was used to represent an autism spectrum disorder. Clinicians used it as an umbrella term that covered a wide range from mild to severe when they weren't sure where the child was on the spectrum. I brought this report to my pediatrician who finally referred me to a developmental pediatrician— an expert in diagnosing autism spectrum disorders. The waiting list was four months long.

The E.N.T. around the same time performed an A.B.R. (Auditory Brain Response) on Jamie to accurately determine hearing function. This test was done under sedation and proved that he had no hearing deficits. This doctor told me with all confidence that Jamie had autism. He actually used the "A" word. He told me he had seen a multitude of children for hearing concerns. He recognized that the ones who passed the A.B.R. were all eventually diagnosed with autism. Once again, I was crushed. It felt like my heart and soul were being destroyed one strike at a time. I eventually quit my job. I couldn't concentrate any longer and found myself helplessly crying in the bathroom during my shifts. I continued to read and research autism and found myself coming to grips with the inevitable.

Soon after this devastating blow, Jamie's appointment with the famous naturopath in town arrived. This guy was a little quirky but seemed to have all the answers. I had read every book I could get my hands on before I entered his office. I told him I was sure my son had all the symptoms of autism. He listened and agreed. He was a wealth of knowledge and had tons of experience treating children with Jamie's symptoms. He reverberated all of the information I had gathered from reading. His expertise was the healthy gluten-free casein-free diet. With his history of long-term antibiotic use, the integrity of Jamie's digestive system had most likely been compromised contributing to the incomplete break down of the proteins found in gluten and casein. The doctor's plan was to maximize Jamie's nutrition by changing his diet and by using dietary supplements including B12 shots. He was also exploring the benefits of chelation. I had primarily gone for the B12 shots that were proving so successful in stimulating language but resolved to put my trust in this doctor and follow his regimen. The diet was stringent, expensive, and difficult to follow. The supplements were astronomical as well, but we followed the course of treatment.

He also addressed detoxification. He explained that due to a genetic predisposition called a MTHFR mutation, that Jamie had a roadblock in his metabolic process causing faulty methylation. MTHFR is a gene that provides instruction for the enzyme responsible for folate metabolism.[1] The MTHFR mutation hinders proper methylation necessary for many important biological functions including repairing DNA, fighting infections, but most importantly detoxification and neurological activity.

By this time, Jamie had received over thirty vaccinations. The strain these toxic vaccinations had placed upon his metabolic pathway was too much. Unable to detoxify properly, he had developed neurological complications.

This seems to explain why, when receiving the same exact vaccinations, some children are a victim of neurological damage, and others are neurotypical. Perhaps children without the gene mutation have a normal metabolic pathway and can clear these toxins without the resulting neurological dysfunction.

My poor little baby drank a sippy cup full of orange juice containing around ten crushed supplements every morning. We also began the vitamin B12 shots three times a week that were so tiny we gave them while he was sleeping.² The speech therapist, who worked with Jamie now three times a week, saw a definite improvement in attention and focus once the shots were started. Beau and I could also see positive changes at home. Jamie appeared to be calmer, had more eye contact, and seemed to communicate with us a little more. I can't say there were earth-shattering changes, only subtle ones. He also had a different look in his eyes.

It was time to call the stuffy lady at the school board back. I did so with my tail between my legs humbly asking for a spot in the developmental preschool program. She was surprisingly nice. We had a big fancy legal meeting with documentation, and he was all set. They even arranged a bus to pick him up and drop him off in front of our house. Jamie, now on the supplement regimen and a strict gluten-free casein-free diet, adjusted nicely. He seemed to enjoy it, and I was pleased and comfortable with the teachers there.

I have to admit, I silently cried every time I saw that handicap bus arrive to pick him up. I was not ashamed— no, not at all. I was just so saddened to see the hard life that lay ahead for my baby. I could see he was pitiful, so vulnerable to this harsh world. I knew his little life would never be normal. I cried often in fear, of the unknown, of what his life would be.

My mother-in-law, "Nana," continued to visit every two weeks. She was such an important part of our children's lives and a welcomed presence in the house. She brought me up many times when I was so low. Her attitude was a blessing. As I would be mourning my baby's loss of a normal life watching the bus approach, she would proceed to climb on that bus and cheerfully take pictures. Later she would marvel about how adorable he looked when he went to school. She had a gift of celebrating the sweet, precious gift that he was to all of us. I learned so much from her.

The day finally arrived when Jamie would get evaluated. Beau went with me to the appointment. Many interventions had been in place before our son's evaluation with the developmental pediatrician. He was on the gluten-free casein-free diet. He was in speech therapy and was on vitamin and mineral supplements, omega 3's, probiotics, digestive enzymes as well as B12 shots three times a week. Beau and I were allowed to observe during the evaluation. We both thought Jamie was having an extraordinarily good day. He was alert and focused. He followed commands and made eye contact. We were very curious as to what the doctor would surmise.

*Chapter Two*
# Adventures in Autism

*"Are you weak and heavy laden, Cumbered with a load of care? Precious Savior still our refuge: Take it to the Lord in prayer."*

— *"What a Friend We Have in Jesus,"*
*Joseph M. Scriven (1855)*

In May of 2005, Jamie was diagnosed with autism. He was four years old. The developmental pediatrician specifically labeled him with Asperger's Syndrome. It was a very generous label. No clinician working with him from this time on would ever agree with this diagnosis.

I remember the conference with the doctor vividly as though it was yesterday. It was weeks after the evaluation, and I walked into his office for the report. There he sat in his white casual suit with his white hair as though he belonged in the Hamptons. I was thinking he was probably one of those old dudes that drove a corvette in a feeble attempt to recapture their youth. Yes, he was relaxed and gave me the diagnosis as he handed me the typed report. So very nonchalantly, he recommended a special school for Jamie and told me he would need speech and occupational therapy. The news came as no shock to me. But a tidal wave of emotions came over me. I became incensed and began to speak what was on my mind.

I asked him what he was doing to educate pediatricians about the signs and symptoms of autism. I continued that I was exhausted from pleading my case with the best pediatricians in town. I admitted that I actually had to persuade the doctors for this referral. I told him that my child, at four years old, was ineligible for early intervention provided by the state now. We would now have to pay out of pocket for every type of therapy, but most importantly, he missed the golden window of opportunity. I asked him if he just sat in that fancy office in his white suit, fat and happy, as the rest of the ignorant pediatricians failed to help these children. I asked him if he ever wondered why it is recommended by the A.M.A. that children receive at least twenty-five doses of vaccinations before their first birthday. Had he ever pondered the risks or the rewards of this? I asked him if he had made it his business to study the biomedical interventions that were emerging as helpful to some children on the spectrum. What was he doing to help? Did he even care that I had been trying to get someone to listen to me for nearly three years? Did he care that my child was four years old, could barely talk, had repetitive nonfunctional behavior, didn't play, and was miserable most of the time? He sat there unaffected by what I was saying, refusing to be targeted. He had no reply.

Of course, I was wrong for blaming him. It is true that when you point a finger at someone, there are three pointing back at you. I was quite guilty myself of holding on to my denial for dear life. He was just doing his job. Nevertheless, years of anguish and questioning my own sanity had surfaced.

The diagnosis was generous indeed, and I questioned him about it. He said, "This child has not been living in a vacuum. It looks like you have worked with him a lot. He appears to have great adaptive skills." He said we were doing a great job with Jamie at home. He remarked that Jamie had some really strong skills solving puzzles and recognizing letters and numbers. It was true. We all knew Jamie was a smart little boy. He was loved and cared for relentlessly. We had even worked on eye contact which was pretty good now. But he was still echolalic (speaking nonfunctional repetitive language) and had the language of an eighteen-month-old at four years old. The doctor painted an optimistic picture, but I was quite skeptical. After all, the man was with my child for an hour. What could he have known about the development of his last four years?

I was mad. Truly, I was. I was mad at my family who more or less called me crazy and down played the struggles I had gone through raising three babies. I was resentful of the chuckling, the eye rolls, and the reprimand I got from many as I desperately attempted to potty train him. I was now mean, mad, and ready to fight. I resented the harsh treatment and attitudes I received. The world appeared to be full of armchair quarterbacks. No one had been on my side. No one's agenda included meeting me on the front line of the battlefield. The anger and resentment came raining down, but it would have to wait. I would have to tuck it in somewhere deep for another time. In no fiber of my being was there an "I told you so." I had no time for such exhausting anger or resentment. I had work to do.

The doctor in the white suit had recommended a special school in the area. It was a private school specifically designed to meet the needs of the child on the autism spectrum. I thoroughly checked it out. The public preschool Jamie was attending was a huge assortment of many special needs and disabilities. I felt that he needed teachers that really knew how to meet his needs socially, academically, and behaviorally. I knew that Jamie was very late to the party at four years old, and there was no time to lose. My faith in people had diminished greatly over the years. I would not trust just anyone with my precious son.

This special school was fantastic. I met with the director whom I truly respected. I was able to see the clear-cut plan in progress. I also appreciated the small class sizes and the low teacher-to-student ratio. This was clearly the perfect school for Jamie. Speech and occupational therapy were also available after school there. It was perfect, but there was only one obstacle—the tuition at this school was a small fortune. I had quit my job at the hospital knowing I would need to be a full-time mom indefinitely. We simply didn't have that kind of money living off of one income.

Beau, the great man of faith he truly is, said, "Let's pray about it." He was on board the minute I told him about the school. He said yes not knowing where the money would come from. In fact, from that moment on, he was faithful to say yes to everything his son needed sparing no cost.

We did pray about it. I was starting to feel some relief that Jamie would finally get the help he needed. We enrolled him in the summer program and managed to pay the tuition for a couple months. I was very relieved and knew he was in a good environment. The teachers were great with Jamie. I finally felt like I was doing something to help him. It was obvious this was the school he needed, and we had to find a way to enroll him for the following year. Financially, it was just impossible. We continued to pray.

Just before the new school year arrived, God answered. Beau was able to cash in some stock from work—just enough to pay the entire year's tuition. We knew this was no ordinary benefit. It was truly a miracle, and we gave God all the thanks and praise.

## The Great Sadness

At this time, Jamie was on vitamin B12 shots, vitamins, minerals, probiotics, fish oils, liquid zinc and a strict gluten- free casein- free diet. Every morning I would wake up at five am and crush all of the supplements to make his orange juice sippy cup. I also would make the daily bread from scratch in the early morning. There was only a couple of brands of gluten-free bread on the market and they were just yucky. I also made almond flour blueberry muffins, pizza crusts, homemade chocolate chip cookies, and pancakes for the freezer. The diet was very difficult to maintain as I would have to drive across town, close to thirty miles, to the nearest *Whole Foods Market* for the ingredients. There was a skeleton supply of gluten-free food and flours at this time in history. It was quite expensive too.

Once, my mini-van broke down on the Katy-freeway in the middle of the summer when it happened to be 104 degrees. As the tow truck arrived, I was sobbing. He thought I was worried about my vehicle. I blubbered that I had 400 dollars' worth of "whole food" in the back, and I was afraid it would spoil. All ended well as Beau arrived saving me and the food. We still laugh about that incident.

Though I was eternally grateful for the opportunity for Jamie to attend the special school, it was far from the house and quite a drive. It was an hour's drive each way, and he attended from 8am to 12pm Monday through Friday. I would buckle the babies in at

7:15 each morning and stayed around to pick him up. It was just too far to drive back and forth. I would take them to the mall and push them around. Sometimes we would find a shady park or go to Mc Donald's. I would stock my van with diapers, cold drinks, and toys. Many times, I would park in the shade at the school, sit on the floor of the van with the air condition running, and play with them. When it was time to pick Jamie up, I would have to rush home to cook his gluten-free casein-free lunch.

I felt like the world revolved around Jamie, and I was terribly worried that my other two would be affected by the sacrifices. It wasn't fair that they had to be raised in the van. For a while, I had Lisbeth enrolled in ice skating lessons a couple times a week at the nearby mall. I would stroll Drew around on these days. It was getting expensive, and I needed a real solution, so I prayed. Once again, God delivered. I finally found a preschool program at our church where I could bring them for about two hours three days a week so they wouldn't have to ride all day in the van. I would bring them late and pick them up early. I was extremely appreciative but soon became very sad.

It was a sadness I could not shake. It was difficult to do, but I hid it from my children. I would laugh, tickle and play with them, but the minute I would drop them off at preschool, I would cry uncontrollably. I can't explain how broken I was inside. It was a fear and loneliness I had never known. I constantly had tears in my eyes and a knot in my stomach. It didn't help that I barely slept and barely ate. I worried about Jamie and couldn't help the anxiety I had about his future. I also felt incredibly sad that my other two children's identity had become members of the "autism intervention team." Although I did feel like the supplements and diet were helping him, he was still so absent from the world. He was still not really conversing, not interested in other children or any sort of play. He was still stimming with the garage doors. On the upside, he was a bit calmer, sleeping better and fully potty trained now. At times he would even follow commands. However, I was still bothered. He was in a class of five children at school. I noticed right away that he was much more affected by this devastating disorder than the others. He seemed more tucked away in his own world. Though his unruly behaviors had definitely calmed down with the dietary interventions, he was still so far away from me.

I had no time for friends. In fact, the sad matter was that I could not handle the strain of any friendship at this time except the occasional phone call from beloved friends back home. Relationships had become a strain and a drain. I was the type of friend that just needed fellowship and a good laugh, sharing in fun times. The only relationships I could enter had to be easy ones. Most people I met with little ones needed help and looked to me knowing I would give anyone the shirt off of my back. The problem was, I no longer had a shirt. So, after several exhausting babysitting gigs and hosting many playdates at my house where I constantly apologized for Jamie's behavior, I simply retreated. I had absolutely nothing to give. No one could reciprocate. No one ever offered. Jamie was a full-time job, and I could barely manage with my own babies. So, I avoided friendships as I came to realize I was in survival mode. I am sure that this isolation contributed to my sadness.

I was also truly overcommitted. Each morning I cooked, fed the babies, prepared supplements, cleaned, changed diapers, dressed my children, did a load of laundry and packed up their stuff for the day before the journey to school. I did a full day's work before 7:30 am every day. After dropping Jamie off at school, I would shop the nearest *Whole Foods Market* for ingredients for this diet which actually seemed to get more complicated with each doctor's visit. Any spare time would be reading any and all literature about autism as I waited in the carpool line. After the journey home, I would fix a gluten-free casein-free lunch and a regular lunch for the other two. The afternoon was dedicated to playing and nurturing all three. (Naps were always a miraculous occurrence.) The evenings revolved around supper, baths, and story time. I put Jamie and Lisbeth in the same room in twin beds so I could read to them both at the same time. I would also read to and rock Drew each night before I put him down.

As I finally made it to bed, I would lay awake and worry about all of the things I should have done. I recall feeling as though each one of my children's entire well-being solely depended on me. I desperately worried about Lisbeth and Drew's development as well as Jamie's. I was concerned about the strain that this intense therapy commitment would place on them. I put myself on trial each night and rarely got more than two to three hours of sleep. If I did fall asleep, I woke up panicked in a cold sweat, then... back to court.

I was, however, immersed in earnest prayer, actually pleading with the Lord to heal my son. I prayed continuously for the Lord to recover my son with diet, supplements, and therapy. I also begged Him to restore my broken soul. My spirit was definitely poor. I used to recite the first beatitude with tears in my eyes as I drove Jamie to school each morning. "Blessed are the poor in spirit, for theirs is the kingdom of heaven" (Matthew 5:3). I prayed all the way there each day listening to my favorite "Hillsong Church" music.

I could never explain how deeply the enemy had me wrapped and bound by the thousand-pound weight that fear, anxiety, and sadness create. I remember thinking if I didn't have this weight, my life wouldn't be nearly as hard. If I could regain my joy— if I could feel like a good mother— if I could just breathe easy for once.

I loved my children with a fervor. Unfortunately, the enemy took advantage of this and tortured me relentlessly.

I had a dream one night that I was physically fighting Satan over my children. He was trying to scare them. I fought and fought with all my might, but he continually laughed at me as though I was a joke. I awoke from that dream burning up in a sweat and ran immediately to comfort Lisbeth who was screaming and crying in her bed. It was very creepy.

Now, as I look back I believe that's exactly what was going on. I was trying to fight the great fight alone. It just wasn't possible. It was a disaster. I needed to count on my Lord to fight all of my battles. As I have come to know Him, He will fight, and He always wins.

He was already fighting for me in ways I could not even see at the time. My marriage was barely hanging on by a single thread called love. Beau and I both resented each other at this time. Life was difficult. I needed things from him that he was unable to give, and he needed me as well. Somehow, we managed to stay united. I believe God singlehandedly held us together at that time. The fact that our marriage survived this storm is a miracle in itself. I did not nurture my marriage. Honesty, I was barely a wife at all. There was simply not enough of me. I did not preserve my marriage; God did.

The Lord carried me through the sadness as well. I noticed that as Jamie started receiving the intervention he needed, I started recovering. I felt a little bit more alive and functional. I started teaching the three to pedal tricycles outside, and we began to socialize with the neighbors. I had a trace of hope that he would, at least in some way, recover from this debilitating state. But I had placed my hope in intervention, not so much in the Lord. This became a problem.

# The Great Interventions

As I drifted in and out of the stages of grief over Jamie's diagnosis, I became obsessed with intervention. I read incessantly about the biomedical causes of autism. As I had very little time to read, I became a speed reader overnight. I read, on average, one book a day during this time and would recite all of the research and very insightful speculation to Beau in the evenings. I was quickly coming to understand some of the contributing factors to this terrible disorder. The biggest contributing factor was a genetic detoxification error. Along with toxins already evident in processed foods, I worried about cooking in foil due to the aluminum. I worried about flame retardant chemicals in the clothing. I saw toxins everywhere, and I was a nervous wreck. It was like I had to hold my mouth right for him to be healed. I felt an enormous amount of pressure.

His diet had to be perfect, according to the naturopath and the research, in order to detoxify his little body. I had to carefully scrutinize every bite he put into his mouth. It seemed like there was very little left to feed him. To help with variety and interest, I tried to substitute all of his favorite foods in gluten- free casein-free sugar-free form. Everything I could not buy at *Whole Foods Market,* I would make myself from scratch. His appetite was just puny, and after a while, he began to lose interest in mealtimes.

At the same time, the naturopath began to suggest chelation therapy. This was a hot topic at the time as the holistic community began to discover high amounts of heavy metals in children on the autism spectrum. (Chelation is the treatment for heavy metal poisoning.) He was suggesting a transdermal cream form of a chelating agent. I knew from research that this was a safer and milder form than the oral or I.V. forms. After much research and careful deliberation, we began to chelate Jamie. It was a putrid cream that we rubbed on his back with a coffee cup three times a week. The poor little fella went to school stinking like brimstone on those days. It did seem that every intervention we added helped him a little bit. Beau and I were definitely seeing improvements, especially in behavior, so we were afraid to stop. We had to see the plan through and follow the doctor's advice as he proved much success completely recovering children with autism.

The teachers at the special school Jamie attended were not impressed. I started to feel like they thought I was wacky. One teacher confronted me with an exasperated tone about his diet, supplements, and chelation therapy a few months later. She fussed at me claiming he was getting worse. "He doesn't act the same, doesn't look the same and doesn't even smell the same." She proceeded, "He is autistic—completely autistic. It is a miracle that you have taught him to speak at all and a miracle that you were able to potty train him. This is his life and your life. You had better accept it as it is, quit these ridiculous therapies and start getting plugged into the autism community who can help you." She basically told me that he would never recover.

I was not offended but panic-stricken. Was I harming him with these therapies? I began to seriously question the chelation therapy and quickly decided to pay a visit to one of the world leading experts on chelating autistic children. She was an M.D. in Baton Rouge, the town in which I was born and spent many years working as a nurse. I made the appointment, brought the babies to Lafayette to stay with Nana, picked up my supportive mother and away we went.

Stephanie Cave M.D. was a doctor in the D.A.N. network. D.A.N. is an acronym for "Defeat Autism Now"— a program started by a great man by the name of Bernard Rimland who had a son with autism. He developed a research institute called "Autism Research Institute" dedicated to the biomedical implications and treatment of autism.[1] Before, as most of us know, autism was considered purely a product of environmental influences, and therefore largely blamed on the mother. This man researched the impact of certain chemical reactions in the brain and successfully concluded that vitamin B6 and magnesium greatly diminished some of the negative autistic behaviors. With this well-established, he looked backwards and came up with many causative factors influencing neurotransmission in the brain. With his research, he concluded that autism was in some way biomedical in origin. He researched many avenues in which to greatly help these children. "Defeat Autism Now," now obsolete, was a method used by many M.D.'s, D. O.'s, and naturopaths trained in his research to ultimately help the brain function in these debilitated children. The method largely relied on healing the gut in order to heal the brain. These doctors also relied heavily on vitamins, supplements, and supporting detoxification to help the child heal. Chelation was quickly becoming part of the plan, and Stephanie Cave was one of the pioneers.

I loved her from the moment I met her. She was down to earth, honest, and she confirmed everything I had been reading about autism. She earnestly prayed for my son and said that that the autism epidemic was spiritual warfare. I totally agreed.

She had been researching biomedical interventions and treating children with success for years when I met her. She had even written a book, which I had read, about a safer immunization schedule.[2] She agreed with me about the vaccinations playing a role in causative factors. She observed high levels of heavy metals from children on the autism spectrum when she provoked them with a chelating agent. Many of these metals included lead, cadmium, and mercury. She was convinced that the preservatives in the vaccinations were not properly excreted in some children due to a genetic mutation. She was an expert in heavy metal chelation— this was the reason for my visit. I trusted her and proceeded with her protocol.

Jamie tested very high for lead. I began oral chelation as recommended and continued to see the naturopath in Houston for diet and nutrition therapy.

Unfortunately, I halted the chelation therapy after a month or so. I did not see him improving or having a healing regression. I became concerned that the sulfur agent was wreaking havoc in his little gut. I prayed about the chelation therapy after the fact and realized this was not the right treatment for Jamie. Had I prayed first and not taken matters in my own hands, I would have known this much sooner.

I still maintain that the work this doctor has done has been courageous and well worth the fight. I certainly agree with her stance on vaccinations and the idea of chelation. She has helped many children drastically with her protocol. However, this is a very complicated matter. I share in the opinion that chelation is most helpful for acute poisonings. Once heavy metals have buried deep into the tissues, it is not as effective. I believe that there are many causes for this brain disorder called "autism." Heavy metal poisoning is just one. I wholeheartedly believe in assisting the body to chelate itself naturally through time, antioxidant rich foods, and gentle supplements. After much prayer, that's what we decided to do with Jamie.

My little boy was on the cutting edge of all reasonable biomedical interventions. I know that all of the healthful measures we took with him helped in some way, especially the diet and supplements. But he was not recovered. A year later I did not see the extraordinary changes I was expecting. He was still in his own little world. I had taken matters in my own hands as though I had the power to help him. I truly thought God was empowering me with all of this vast knowledge so that I could restore my little boy. I was devastated when I candidly reflected and felt that he was no better off. He had been poked and prodded, seen by so many doctors, deprived of yummy kid food, and made to drink countless supplements. I was overwhelmingly sad and disappointed. Most of all I felt guilty for putting little Jamie and the rest of my family through such a difficult ordeal. I felt sorry for Beau, who lovingly and generously handed over our last few bucks for all of these treatments.

Yes, I cried and prayed for a while, felt very remorseful, and openly admitted failure. I put Jamie back on a regular diet and just concentrated on loving, playing, and teaching. I surrendered him to the Almighty and finally felt sixteen tons released from my shoulders. I felt the freedom that comes with "letting go and letting God,"— for a little while, that is.

Jamie completely tanked on a regular diet including treats and an occasional *Mc Donald's* Happy Meal. His behaviors and moods were taking a turn for the worse. Beau and I knew we had to resume his diet, but this time we wanted him to enjoy his food and feel like a regular kid. We toyed around with a healthful whole foods diet and tried to implement this without too many restrictions. I would bake regular bread so it would not have any preservatives. I would also make his favorite dish, macaroni and cheese, from scratch as well as homemade chocolate chip cookies and pies. Sugar proved to be poison to him, so I had to eliminate it when possible. I felt certain that the reintroduction of wheat and milk products were still a problem, but I was compelled to let go for a while. There was no misunderstanding; diet was an important piece to the puzzle.

# The Perils of Diet

My first revelation of the relationship between food and behavior came after reading Karyn Seroussi's book "Unraveling the Mystery of Autism and Pervasive Developmental Disorder."[3] I knew Jamie was on the autism spectrum way before he was diagnosed and searched endlessly for answers. I remember clearly one evening, I escaped from home to browse around the local bookstore. I was praying for God to direct me and provide me with a way to help my little boy. When I picked up this book, I knew God had placed it in my hands. I read it and believed it knowing that I had found truth.

The basis of her book is implementing the gluten-free casein-free diet in order to heal the gut, and therefore heal the brain. The biochemical evidence of this principal is clearly outlined. In a nutshell, when an individual has a damaged intestinal lining, otherwise known as a "leaky gut," the inability to properly digest wheat and milk proteins creates toxic chemical byproducts (urinary peptides) which cross the blood- brain barrier creating a condition similar to an opioid response. This is the basis of Dr. Kalle Reichelt's "Opioid Excess" theory explained very coherently in Seroussi's book.[4]

It seems quite ironic and comical to me today that I see the pharmaceutical companies now actually promoting a new drug for the obese population addressing this very theory. The new miracle drug is none other than the oral form of the narcotic antagonist we used in the emergency room to recover patients from an opioid overdose. This drug is a common staple of any "crash cart" in any hospital. It seems to me the premise of the medication is to alleviate food addiction by eliminating the "euphoric high" that comes with the incomplete digestion of certain proteins. This is a very powerful drug. In my experience, patients have literally flown off the table after its intravenous administration. Where is the prudence and forthright responsibility that we expect of our pharmaceutical companies? One would be compelled to think dietary changes in this instance would seem to be more appropriate. Nevertheless, these drug companies have certainly validated Reichelt's theory.

I can't pretend to be an expert on the biochemical aspect of autism, but I can give some pretty strong and noteworthy opinions on the matter based upon the reality and experiences in our home. I truly believe, to this day, in healing the gut to heal the brain.

Some of the common side effects we noticed in Jamie, as we kept a food diary, were episodes of intoxication as like with alcohol. He would display maniacal laughter with naughtiness, spaciness, and incoherence. The end result was an alteration in his reality. How can one possibly function in a school setting, make appropriate peer relationships, or communicate effectively at all if their reality is altered?

The gut-brain discovery is not new, and it is still quite a huge piece of the autism puzzle, especially where behavior is concerned.

Knowing that Jamie had all of these food sensitivities, one would ask why we took him off the diet. After all, we had evidence it was helping. There are many reasons. First, I was counting on his digestive tract being healed as he had been on the diet for quite some time now. He wasn't eating enough, and he was showing less than average growth patterns at the pediatrician's office. Also, the restrictions put a great strain on Jamie and the rest of the family. But most of all, I believed God had an easier plan. I had gone to a national autism conference and had listened to a lecture on "whole foods." Diet was an important part of the healing process, but the child had to grow. This plan was reasonable, and this is what we decided to do. We fed him the healthiest foods we could barring chemicals and preservatives. Keeping him entirely off of processed sugar helped most of all.

It would take years before I stopped the D.A.N. protocol. In fact, Jamie had seen D.A.N. doctors in three different states before I halted. I still believe in the research behind it and the principals involved. It is very intricate, and it is important to remember that each child is an individual. What works for one child will not necessarily work for another. I am thankful for the progress we made with Jamie during this time, but God lets you know when it's time to move on.

Though we ended the D.A.N. protocol, the intervention frenzy did not stop. Over the course of the next five years we tried, in addition to speech and occupational therapy, A.I.T. (A program where Jamie would listen to filtered classical music through very expensive headphones), N.A.E.T. (Nambudripad's Allery Elimination Techniques) to help with food allergies, homeopathy, acupuncture, cranio-sacral therapy, the Specific Carbohydrate diet, the Maker's diet, and yeast elimination programs designed by our nutritionist. The only thing left to do was to dance naked around a campfire chanting and rubbing chicken bones together. I absolutely refused to do that.

Aside from alternative therapies, we had Jamie enrolled in swimming lessons, karate and social groups for several years. He also underwent Applied Behavior Analysis therapy, vision therapy, completed a Learning Rx program, and later attended Sylvan Learning Center. We also hired private tutors to help him with reading.

Though they were all exhausting physically and financially, I know that each one of these therapies was helpful. It took a long time for Beau and I to see any clear-cut progress. We got discouraged, broke, tired, and cranky along the way. After all, we still had two other children that needed love and attention. Lisbeth and Drew became involved in ballet, piano, and t-ball, among many other activities. This was a very precious time in our family's life. I wouldn't regret it for a minute. But life was challenging at this time. It took a toll on me in many ways, so much that my health started to fail.

By the time Jamie was seven, I had completely exhausted my body. I felt bad nearly all of the time. I was only thirty-seven years old, and my body ached like a feeble little old lady as I got out of bed each morning. My knees throbbed as I would climb the stairs, and I basically felt like I had been hit by a Mack truck every day. My blood pressure was consistently 80/55, mostly likely the reason I was so tired and short of breath.

I eventually found a chronic fatigue clinic that was indeed a money hemorrhage but did treat my anemia, nearly absent cortisol levels and low thyroid. I had exhausted my adrenal glands from years of stress, poor diet, and no sleep. Though I have been known to roll my eyes at many of these clinics, I have to say I was grateful for the help I received. After about six months of treatment, I felt good again. Appreciating my regained health and vitality, I started exercising regularly, eating correctly, and I was finally able to sleep.

What I learned is that God's plan is so much easier than ours. Jesus said, "My yoke is easy and my burden is light" (Matthew 11:30). The truth is I took on insurmountable burdens every day for years. They were burdens that I placed upon myself as I, subconsciously, continued to blame myself for my son's heartbreaking disability. It is easy to see now how little faith I had in my Heavenly Father. My lack of faith cost me my health and much more. God never intended for me to live as a prisoner in a concentration camp. This was never God's plan. God's plan was to restore Jamie in accordance with His will and on His own time to bring about the fullness of His kingdom; and He didn't need my help.

## Chapter Three
# New Beginnings and Bad Behaviors

*"When peace, like a river attendeth my way, when sorrows like sea billows roll, whatever my lot, Thou hast taught me to say, It is well, it is well with my soul."*

— *"It is Well with My Soul," Horatio Spafford (1873)*

In June of 2006, Beau was transferred, and our family got the unique opportunity to move to the most beautiful city in the world— Denver, Colorado. It was a move we welcomed. We moved to a beautiful picturesque suburb south of the city. The views of the mountains were amazing, and the air was crisp and clean. The sun, in all its glory, exuded pure happiness.

We moved into a quaint "fixer upper" on a nice cul-de sac. Our house backed to open space and open sky with mountain views.

The neighborhood was filled with friendly neighbors and children. It felt like a fresh start. Beau and I were beyond happy. Jamie was five, Lisbeth was three, and Drew was two.

Following our move to Denver, Jamie was still very speech delayed and antisocial. He did not seem to be interested in playing with the other children. He roamed around and perseverated on everyone's garage doors. I cannot imagine how hard the change must have been on him. He had several meltdowns a day and crawled in bed with me every morning at 3am. All I remember wanting at that time was to see him squeal with excitement. My other two children were making friends and adjusting beautifully. I spent a lot of time trying to assimilate Jamie into the neighborhood action. I asked the children to include him and stayed close by to help him be appropriate. Sadly, he had very little interest in anything. My heart ached that he was so trapped inside himself that he could not experience the joys of childhood. Still, I was determined to remain optimistic.

I had my hands full, and I had my heart full. I wanted so much for my family. I also wanted to be a loving, caring neighbor. I wanted to be someone everyone could count on. I opened my home and my heart to everyone and treasured this sense of community. I loved sledding and making snow forts with all of the neighborhood kids, flying kites, biking to the park and hiking to the creek. I mostly loved sitting on our front porch in the evening visiting with everyone. It was a magical time. I had all that I ever wanted— a happy, healthy family.

The move to Denver truly helped to usher me out of my sadness. The neighbors were kind and friendly. The children were sweet and accepting. The weather was gorgeous, and the beautiful scenery reminded me of God's greatness and glory every single day. We backed up to a greenbelt that winded through beautiful creeks and meadows one way, and to a lovely park the other. We spent most of our time outside playing. I felt like we were part of a community for the first time, and I began to feel a sense of normalcy.

Due to the fact that Jamie was five and school age, I quickly realized that there were no options but to enroll him in public kindergarten. There were no special schools anywhere in the vicinity, and private schools were not equipped to meet his needs. I was surprised to find that the neighborhood elementary school was more than able and willing to help Jamie. The special needs director was amazing. She knew exactly what he needed and was quick to point out his strengths. The kindergarten teacher was fabulous, and the children in his class were extraordinarily sweet. The atmosphere of the school was positive and community oriented. I had to pinch myself. Jamie was definitely in a good place.

Jamie was still highly affected by autism, and there were no quick fixes or cures which I was discovering the hard way, but he was in a thriving environment. I wish I could have seen all of these blessings at the time, nevertheless, I was still heavily burdened with fear. He was still far submerged into his own world. But looking back, I can see the slow progress he was making.

He began asking everyone when their birthday was and reminded them of it every time he saw them. It was quite a conversation starter. People, adults, and children alike, were amazed and flattered that he could remember such personal details. They loved it. In fact, one day the garbage man came to empty our cans in the back of his truck, and Jamie shouted out his birthday. This guy smiled bigger than Dallas and made small talk. It was obvious that Jamie had made his day. Jamie had humanized this man. He wasn't just a garbage man. He was unique. He was important.

Jamie made strides in kindergarten. He learned his sight words as well as the other children, but he still had a mountain of sensory issues and attention problems. He was very socially limited as well. He would interact for about five minutes at a time, at most. Though often aloof and stuck in his own world, his behaviors were also an issue at times. He could be rude and did not know how to handle frustration. Throwing his shoes or yelling seemed like the right way to get his point across at times. However, everyone loved him. He was adorable and genuine. He had very special para-professionals (trained teacher aides) that helped him in class. I felt like the school rallied around him, guarded him, protected him, and cheered him on.

One of the most unforgettable times that year was his sixth birthday. Jamie was born at the end of March, and people who live in Colorado know that the weather can be very unpredictable in the spring. (It is quite necessary to leave your snow boots next to your flip flops by the door.) I had planned his birthday party at the nearby park due to the gorgeous weather we were having and the fact that I had invited his entire kindergarten class. As luck would have it, we had a huge snow storm that Saturday, and my house just wasn't big enough to fit twenty-five kids. I was in a bind that morning. I decided to phone every child in the class and ask that we move the party to the next day as the weather was predicted to be 65 degrees and sunny. I still find it amazing that every child but one showed up at Jamie's party the next day. Beau's parents came for the occasion as well. The weather was perfect. It was wonderful —a most memorable birthday party.

Jamie was slowly making progress. He loved to jump on our trampoline with the neighborhood kids, and that began his slow ascent into the social world. Eventually, he would ride an old scooter up and down the sidewalks. This too was a big deal because he essentially had no interests other than garage doors. (Speaking of garage doors, we had to physically move our garage door button so high he could not reach it or he would press it continuously.)

It was during this time that he started speech therapy with the best therapist I have ever known. Margo Ames was phenomenal and taught me so much. She focused relentlessly on auditory processing. When Jamie started, he had very little communications skills, just voicing basic needs. He simply could not put words together with pictures. She taught me to play the clue game where I would describe something with clues, and he would have to guess what it was. This forced him to put words together with pictures. She also had us play the game *Guess Who* with Jamie. There are many ways she shared with us how to help his processing.

He was also in OT (occupational therapy) which helped him with sensory issues, something he needed desperately. The main thing that helped Jamie with his sensory issues was our contribution at home. Really, no child is going to overcome this problem with therapy once a week. Beau and I implemented a sensory diet at home. It was not hard either. We just incorporated these fun activities into his daily life. Some things we did involved swinging, blowing bubbles, playing with playdough, digging in the sandbox, running uphill, playing "wheelbarrow," teaching him to do somersaults in the grass, having him pull Drew in the wagon, climbing trees, and pedaling a bike. Nothing was complicated or difficult. We just had to spend a lot of time getting his body adjusted to gravity and space. These activities stimulated his sensory system enabling him to process information. We also had him in karate and swimming lessons that I do believe helped. The OT also taught me the Wilbarger brushing protocol which really calmed him down.[1]

God had another blessing in store for us. By His grace, I was introduced to Ellen and Richard, the sweetest and most helpful older couple with a long history of educating and tutoring struggling kids. Jamie was six when I first brought him for the initial evaluation at their home where they worked. I was to drop him off for an hour and a half. I'll never forget Ellen meeting me on the driveway as I showed up early. She took my face in her hands lovingly, and then kissed my cheek. She said something that went like this, "You poor darling. You need to understand that your child has severe autism and I don't know how much we will be able to help him. You are going to have to come to grips with his disability somehow." My heart sank and my hopes were dashed once more. But what else is left if you have no hope? I had to keep it alive. It's all that I had for him. My hope had to be enough. I did not believe her with all of her good intentions.

She continued to counsel me many times over the next two years about the acceptance of Jamie's diagnosis. She kept trying to prepare me for the inevitable; he would never have any semblance of a normal life. I knew she was coming from a place of love and concern. I politely smiled and nodded but inwardly kept repeating in my head, "Lady, you don't know my son, and you certainly don't know me." I did a lot of things that could be considered silly or pointless at that time, and I made a ton of mistakes, but the one thing I did not do was roll over and play dead.

Richard was incredible and faithfully worked with Jamie once a week. He was very much invested in Jamie, had a tailored unique approach for right-brained students, and had the patience of Job. I can't say that Jamie progressed a lot as nothing really resonated with him at that time. However, Richard and Ellen were both wonderful to me and my son. How I loved and trusted these people. I know that Jamie was blessed by the relationship he had with this kind man.

First grade was wonderful, and I witnessed tons of progress. He simply had the best first grade teacher in the world and his own personal para (teacher's helper) who loved him beyond belief. She accompanied him in the classroom. He was mainstreamed with the utmost success. He was behaving nicely in class and participating more than ever. He was calm and polite. I worked with him on his homework every single night. I could see how difficult reading was for him, but we pushed through.

Some great interventions were put into place at this school by the caring and thoughtful teachers Jamie was blessed to have. Miss G., his paraprofessional (teacher's aide), put together a pamphlet with Jamie's picture on it. It was a little trifold that explained autism, some of the unusual characteristics, and how Jamie manifested his disability. She handed them out to the children in his class. In very simple language, it explained Jamie's behaviors and mannerisms to help his schoolmates understand and become more accepting and tolerant.

She also recognized how loud and chaotic the lunchroom was. She could see it overwhelmed Jamie's senses and implemented "Lunch Bunch" for him. It was simply a quiet lunch in the classroom with one voluntary friend each day. It helped tremendously, and he loved it.

He was doing remarkably well, but I must admit, this was round two of biomedical interventions. I had attended an inspiring conference over the summer and was ready for the challenge. I had him on the Specific Carbohydrate diet, where I made a special, healing homemade yogurt, and many supplements including probiotics, vitamins, minerals, glutathione, and amino acids.[2]

As usual with special diets, around the second half of the year Jamie started losing weight, and his appetite decreased. Being well aware of the definition of insanity, I once again had to expand his diet. Also, his beloved para had been diagnosed with breast cancer and took leave as she had intense chemotherapy and treatment for the rest of the year. Jamie missed her terribly. There were different personalities working with him now, and he was pulled out of the classroom quite often. Many variables were at play, but his behavior definitely changed for the worse. I was so disheartened and felt so sorry for him. He spent the rest of the year mostly outside the classroom where his tension mounted.

Beau and I lobbied heavily before the next school year to have him held back for another year in first grade. He was not reading well, and we felt like to push him through would be a big mistake. We were convinced that if he had another year in first grade to master these needed skills, he would be successful in second grade. His first grade teacher, who loved him, actually suggested it, but we were strongly cautioned against this and ended up listening to the principal and the other faculty regarding this matter. Although we disagreed, we acquiesced to their point of view.

During the summer before second grade we implemented many interventions to help Jamie. We began a program at *Learning Rx* that was quite a commitment in regards to both money and time. It proved to be a beneficial program. I sat with him for an hour each day and was quite impressed. We were very pleased that he had begun to attend to the tasks and cooperate. He also continued with swimming lessons as well as speech, occupational therapy, and social skill classes. I tried so hard to keep him engaged and out of trouble.

As he started emerging from his own little world, we started seeing some obstinate, attention seeking behavior. Of course, Beau and I employed a behavior specialist at this time to help us manage Jamie's behavior. He instituted a behavior log which I kept faithfully. He also created charts and rewards in the light of positive reinforcement. It was time consuming and hard to maintain along with ministering to the needs of my other two children who were five and six. They were now starting to resent all of the time we were spending on Jamie, responding with some bad behaviors of their own.

Jamie was also still very language delayed and at this time still heavily perseverated on garage doors. Once I took him to *Target* where he broke free from my hand and ran to the shoes. He immediately dumped the shoes out of their box, sat Indian style on the cold, hard floor and began to simulate a garage door with the shoebox and the lid.

One of the first things I did upon moving into the neighborhood was to try to reach out to the families as I would meet them and explain Jamie's autism. I wanted them to be aware for safety reasons and to understand that we were very engaged and dedicated to helping him. I was hoping to stoke a little compassion and to evade a few insults and minor complaints. Most of the neighbors were very kind and compassionate, but a few did not understand his fascination with garage doors no matter how hard I tried to explain. Sometimes he would stand and stare at the garage doors going up and down as the cars pulled in. I couldn't hear the snickers and sneers, but I could feel them.

Once, during this summer before second grade, he made little scratches using a screwdriver on a couple of panes on a neighbor's garage door. I was school supply shopping that Sunday and left the children with their father. When I returned and saw what happened, I immediately started to rectify the situation. I rang the doorbell and apologized to the family living there. I assured them that I would have the door professionally painted as soon as possible. I also reassured them we would keep a better eye on Jamie in the future.

I knew the family that lived there as our kids played together. I felt that we could settle this pretty easily knowing that I had spoken to the mother at length about Jamie's behavior plan during that summer. She was aware that we had employed a behavioral therapist and that we were trying.

Unfortunately, she stewed on it all overnight and became incensed. The next day she spoke to Beau. Obviously quite irate, she threatened to call the authorities claiming our son was dangerous. She expressed concern that we let him run around the neighborhood with a screwdriver. She also questioned what kind of parents we were. Beau, very nicely, tried to explain to her that Jamie had never once been a danger to anyone. He was only obsessed with garage doors and told us that he was trying to make a row of windows on hers.

Her garage door was painted within three days looking better than before. I was very upset at her claims against my sweet family. I knew it was completely unwarranted. We had only been super kind and generous to every member of hers. I trusted her. I was quite shocked by her reaction because she knew us quite well. It seemed to me that she trusted us enough to let her daughter spend the entire summer playing at our house. I felt betrayed and extremely hurt by the whole incident.

I realized at that point that I could not let Jamie out of my sight. By now, I was getting accustomed to being fussed and scoffed at. For it is true we had some of the sweetest and kindest neighbors in the world who looked out for and loved our family, but I knew for a fact there were some that didn't even want him walking across their lawn. I became a little angry and bitter but most of all— I felt helpless. I felt like I was fighting this major battle for my son all alone.

He was a precious, affectionate boy that was just doing his best to be noticed and have significance in the world. On a good day, he would dress up in a spider man costume along with his baby brother, jump on the trampoline, and run around the back yard. He also loved to pull his brother in the wagon up the street pretending to take him to "feed the ducks at the pond." I'm quite sure some of the neighbors thought he was really affected as he would pretend to throw food to the ducks. Sadly, no one knew what I knew about him. Many times, while washing dishes in the kitchen, I would peer out the window that overlooked our backyard and see him gesture to me "I love you" in sign language as he was swinging. He was Jamie, definitely unlike all the other little boys his age, but extraordinarily tender and full of love.

Second grade was a difficult year mainly because the school had implemented a significant needs room where children with various needs could enjoy an easier, sensory friendly environment. (It was cost effective as well.) I didn't know it at the time, but this is the worst possible thing that could have ever happened to Jamie. Though the teachers were wonderful and displayed love and compassion for all the kids, expectations were lowered and Jamie fell further behind academically. His behaviors also worsened due to the fact that he felt segregated from his friends. I did not understand this then as I do now. I just knew that my son was not learning, and he took a turn for the worse. He started cussing and laughing at people. He would also try to hurt people's feelings on purpose. He thought it was hilarious. I was deathly concerned. I even prayed over him at night fearing demonic oppression or something. It felt as though a spiritual battle was taking place. There seemed to be an endless cycle of bad behavior, negative consequences, escalating bad behavior, punishment, and so on. Drama in the neighborhood was heating up as well.

The neighborhood kids were getting tired of his attention seeking behavior. While they would play ball, he would grab the ball and run away with it. He would often sabotage their games and repeat things over and over to annoy them. I did all I could to get him involved in the games or give him some sort of role, but he refused. He was not yet ready to participate. The most detrimental thing he was learning at this time was to get attention through obstinate behavior. This was a successful tactic he used at school and at home. He would throw rocks down the sewer. He would take newspapers off of the neighbor's driveway, pick their pretty flowers, and break their decorations. I was always supervising him, but we lived in such close proximity on a quiet cul-de-sac that he would slip away for a good ten minutes every now and then just long enough to get us both in trouble. It felt like he was really becoming a nuisance to everyone, and I noticed that attitudes were no longer tolerant and cheerful. I started having some of the teenagers help me keep an eye on him as well as inviting everyone to play at my house so that I could watch him. I began to keep a tight rein on him, but this too broke my heart. He was a precious little boy that just wanted to be included. He didn't know how to play. And because I was not a peer, he would not let me teach him under any circumstances. I was no substitute for the neighborhood kids. I faithfully tried. The truth was that there was nothing more that I could do to make the neighborhood kids give him a chance, so I continued to pray earnestly and continuously for God to help me help my little boy.

One day out of the blue, my dear friend Miss G., Jamie's beloved paraprofessional at school, had given me a copy of a book titled *A*

*Friend Like Henry.*[3] It was a captivating true story of an autistic boy who was brought out of his lonely world by a very special dog. Of course, it touched me deeply, and I began to think, "If only Jamie had a dog." I would soon talk my husband into getting a dog for our lonely little boy. This was not a victory easily won.

I researched and sought out the right dog for Jamie and the rest of the family. At Christmastime during his second-grade year, Jamie had a sweet little Spaniel/Bischon mix female who he named Mabel. She was special all right. She had the best temperament of any dog I have ever known. She was extraordinarily gentle, playful, and looked you straight in the eyes. She seemed to understand everything we were saying and followed commands automatically. She lived to play. Beau and I would laugh hysterically as she would jump on our trampoline with the boys playfully pulling their pants down with her teeth. She would gleefully sled with the kids and even canoed and camped with us. She was always game for anything and everything. She didn't have a mean bone in her body and trusted us all implicitly. She was highly intelligent, learned tricks with ease, loved to snuggle, and being so very crafty, always found a way to get to our food.

She was an amazing little dog, but she was mine from the first time I picked her up. It was certainly not meant to happen that way. I wanted her to be Jamie's special dog. I wanted her to give him company and joy, filling the lonely void in his life. I wanted him to bond with her, feeling unconditional love and loyalty. Without a doubt, he did love her and enjoy her immensely. He played with her and would help me bathe her. He learned to feed her and enjoyed walking her. I know in my heart she certainly brought blessings to his life, but it was obvious to everyone she was my dog. Years later I came to realize that God brought her to me, not Jamie. I figure He knew how much I needed her. Yes,

God gave me a dog—the sweetest dog in the world. She has been one of the great loves of my life. She still, to this day, brings me comfort and joy like no person could.

As much as we all loved this sweet little dog who brought so much life into our home, my little boy was still lonely. He had no friends, no interests and often declined to spend time with me. But I could not leave him alone to constantly stim (using solitude and mindless, stereotypical behaviors to reduce anxiety). This would be detrimental and I knew it.

I did my best to keep him involved in every fun activity I could think of. It was a constant battle keeping him engaged and interactive. We began to have regular tea parties in Lisbeth's room. He actually participated and seemed to enjoy them. This was a great opportunity to vicariously teach manners. I would also take him to the park to ride his scooter, play on the equipment and fly kites. I would make sure to bring as many neighborhood kids along as possible. This way, he could at least watch them play ball and interact. I usually kept a posse around Jamie in hopes that he could learn through observation, but this also entailed a lot of griping and complaining. All he knew how to do was annoy kids for attention.

I never stopped trying to involve Jamie in the mix of things. I would not stand for him to be left out. Once, Lisbeth and her friend employed my help to make a Lemonade stand on the corner of the street. I was all too happy to set them up, but they refused to let Jamie and Drew participate. This was a problem I could easily solve. As they were selling lemonade for twenty-five cents a cup, I made a "Tang" stand on the other corner for my boys selling at ten cents a cup. The people that stopped by laughed and laughed and were kind to buy a cup from each.

I could see how lonely my son was, and I faithfully prayed for God to tell me what I could do. I soon received an idea as summer rolled around. I printed up a flyer and put it on the church's bulletin board. It read, "Special Friend Needed for Special Little Boy." I was advertising for a twelve or thirteen-year-old boy to come over to our house and play with Jamie. I thought an older kid would be more patient and be able to mentor him. I was offering to pick him up, pay him, and bring him home during the summer. In blind faith, I did this. I certainly did not have the money or the time but did it anyway, knowing it was God's idea, not mine.

I was delighted that there were many inquiries. We ended up with a precious friend named Marcos. He really took time with Jamie and was kind to all of my children. We would pick him up for a few hours three times a week. He gave me a much-needed respite while spending valuable time with Jamie. Marcos was a blessing to us all that summer. It was one of those few things that actually worked out, and I have God to thank.

As we muddled through the plethora of behavioral issues and neighborhood drama that summer, we were also fighting the age-old school battle. For the parent of a child with autism it goes like this, "Our child is not learning, and he needs one-on-one instruction." And then the school's response through their actions is:

"But we don't have enough money."

After second grade, Beau and I were completely distraught with where Jamie was. We actually thought he was getting worse in every way: attitude, behavior, and academics. We were adamant that he receive the opportunity to repeat second grade as he was still not reading. I even requested that the autism team from the district come to evaluate his program at school. They were quite impressed with the interventions and gave a glowing report.

Yes, the teachers had wonderful attitudes and dealt with behaviors like champions. But throwing out a couple of worksheets throughout the day was not cutting it. It was more like an enrichment program. He was not learning enough, he was not progressing, and he was getting further behind academically every day. His behaviors had certainly gotten much worse, and he had started using bad language. He was quite amused when the teachers showed any sort of negative reaction to his shenanigans. I felt helpless.

After many meetings with the school educators that summer including the principal, we were turned down. This was a good school with great faculty. I held them all in high esteem. My only complaint was that Jamie needed more time. But as we soon found out, schools no longer hold children back. They claimed it would not benefit him, only diminish his self-esteem. I was convinced it was all about district money.

The claim that another year would not benefit him really had me miffed. I got the impression that the administration did not think that Jamie was capable of remediation. No, I did not like this in a box. I did not like this with a fox—not in the rain, or on a train. I immediately searched for a not for profit parent advocacy service in the area. I wanted to know our rights.

Beau and I soon met with a local nonprofit parent advocate who cared about nothing more than his IQ scores. (Yep they were super low.) She showed us graphs and statistics proving that Jamie's potential was low, and this potential does not change with age or any interventions. She agreed with the school, that holding Jamie back would be a futile effort. She basically gave me the same speech Ellen had but very smug and with much less love.

Momma was not happy. Keeping my temper in check I asked her, "How can you possibly measure the potential of a child or anyone of that matter?" I let her know that my child was indeed capable of learning. I gently schooled her for a moment on the human spirit, her attitude, and God's provision; then we left.

Autism is a different animal. It is a new age disability that many of the so called "experts" know nothing about. You cannot and should not test a child on the spectrum for his I.Q. It is detrimental. It limits our children. That's all it does. It gives us as parents and teachers the okay to roll out the baskets so in desperate need of weaving.

Jeffrey Freed in his book *"Right-Brained Children in a Left-Brained world,"* who maintains that all children on the autism spectrum are right-brain learners, says, "Right- brained children are generally at a disadvantage in timed IQ testing situations because they need more time to turn the visual pictures in their minds into the written answers required on a test." He continues, "Until a far better test is devised...we should put IQ tests on the back burner. They are subjective, shaming, and often a deterrent, keeping students from following their dreams—the last thing they need."[4]

Ken Robinson also points out in his book *Creative Schools* that, "It (the IQ score) presents a narrow and misleading conception of how rich and diverse human intelligence really is."[5] These were my thoughts exactly. I could not put limits on my son.

In the dark of night with only the moonlight shining through his window, I would snuggle next to him in his little bed before he fell asleep, and we would talk. It was so quiet you could hear a pin drop. It was peaceful and void of distractions. The conversations I had with my sweet boy were profound and meaningful. He was comfortable and out of "fight or flight" mode, the one he operated on during the day to cope with the sensory nightmare of school and life in general. I enjoyed the time I had to reassure him about how much he was loved and valued. It seemed I was continuously correcting him with my patience at an all time low by the end of every day. I loved being able to fill his little bucket back up with love and encouragement.

We talked about school and friends. Answering my questions, he was finally able to give me a little glimpse into his world. I was floored one night as he asked me, "Mommy, who made God?" He was much more capable than anyone could ever know. In this environment he was able to show me what I always knew in my heart— he definitely had potential. I did not care to what extent. I just wanted to nurture it any way I could.

I felt as though no one saw Jamie as capable of learning. He was inattentive to almost every effort and was now becoming naughty as well. I did understand why educators formed this opinion and knew that they were shooting me straight. But my thoughts were something like this… "What if he is just developmentally slow? What if one day his senses, intellect, and emotions all rectify and start working together and he is as capable as anyone? What if we are sentencing him to a life void of meaningful education before his life even begins? What if all he needs is time?" This would certainly be a tragedy and not something I could ever live with being his mother. I had to believe in him at all costs. I didn't care if we had to "fake it" before he could "make it." It would certainly be better than facing my son one day with the fact that I never believed in his God given potential.

Now, in the instance that he would never be capable of real learning, mature responsibility or meaningful relationships, I would graciously concede knowing I had done everything humanly possible. In this reality, I could surely live with myself and happily accept my beautiful son as he was.

Beau and I reluctantly accepted the fact that he would be forced to move along to the third grade without being able to read. We were not so much disappointed in the school as we were the system. Needless to say, I had no peace with this, and I was forced to have a faith in the system.

Jamie began third grade in the special needs room once more, with an occasional outing to his regular homeroom classroom in order to meet IEP (Individual Education Plan—a legal document used to aid students with disabilities) requirements. I was beginning to see that sitting in a regular classroom without the appropriate modifications was also futile. He was far behind now, and he would be better served in the special needs room if someone would take the time and initiative to put him on a tailored, progressive, learning curriculum. But I was done fighting with the school. I was done with IEP's. I was done with the experts at the district level who actually thought they had a clue about teaching a child on the spectrum. But most of all, I was tired of no one giving my child the opportunity to be properly educated.

By Christmastime, I still wasn't seeing Jamie progress. He was not coming home with readers or homework. His time was spent predominantly in the special needs room counting money and working on handwriting. There was still no one reading with him one-on-one which I thought was the main priority. I tried to read with him every night, but he was usually so spent from being at school all day and therapy all afternoon that he just didn't have anything left.

He was not very compliant, and I didn't feel right strong-arming him. I was in tune to separating his "won'ts" from his "can'ts." This was a "can't." I was soon realizing that he was not able to read with me after a long day of school and therapy. If I just had him when he was fresh, I would read with him and work with him like crazy. He needed intense direct instruction. The expense to hire someone to do this at home was not something we could afford. We lived paycheck to paycheck paying out of pocket for all his therapy as it was.

I was now becoming disgruntled with public school. Jamie still could not read…at all. His behaviors were getting worse by the day. My heart was breaking as I knew he was getting a bad reputation at school. I saw kids that used to be kind and patient with him pushing him away as they were getting aggravated by his antics. I laid awake at night visualizing Jamie lying in a pool of algae, stagnate, being consumed with amoebas and gunk due to the lack of activity. As Bob Marley played in my head, I decided come what may, I was going to stir it up. I may not do it right, but I knew I would do something. I felt we had nothing to lose and everything to gain.

After Christmas break, I pulled Jamie out of third grade and began homeschooling him using the *Abeka* first grade curriculum. It was quite a chore. He was not easy to work with. He could not attend to the work, he could not follow instructions, and aside from a few sight words, he could not read. He had no imagination or motivation as he had very few interests.

One day he locked himself in the bathroom and unraveled about ten rolls of toilet paper out all over the place. When he opened the door all I saw was a white fluff with some little blue eyes staring back. I started cracking up laughing, then so did he. I sat on the bathroom floor giggling with him and holding him and kissing him until I started sobbing.

He also smashed one of Lisbeth's water globes into a million pieces one day when I sent him to his room for time out. More than anything, he hated being reprimanded. There was nothing easy about this task. I started developing a lot of empathy for the teachers at school. Then God sent me to Julie.

I received an email from the Autism Society advertising a free one-night seminar taught by an A.B.A. therapist highlighting behaviors that hinder learning. I had always longed for Jamie to receive A.B.A therapy but knew that we could never in a million years bear the cost.

Applied Behavior Analysis is a therapy that is tried and true in the autism world. A highly-trained therapist utilizes the function of behavior to work with the child using rewards through discrete trials in an understanding that behavior is a response to the environment.[6] As far as I knew, A.B.A. therapy was only for the very rich or the very poor.

I drove downtown that bitterly cold, dark night, and miraculously found my way. As I intently listened to her that evening, I knew she was the one to help. She met with me after the seminar, and we set up an appointment for an evaluation.

Totally competent, professional, and brilliant was the girl from England. She came to the house and worked with Jamie about six hours a week. She gave us a discounted price since we did not qualify for financial assistance. Our parents generously helped out so we could make it happen.

She was incredible, and in the spirit of the old Chinese saying, started "teaching me to fish." Her aim was training parents to deal correctly with unwanted behaviors, promoting cooperation and compliance which is necessary for any real learning to take place.

She strongly maintained that Jamie should have never been placed in a significant needs room. He should have been in the regular classroom with behavioral and academic expectations. There was no doubt in her mind that my child was capable of learning. She claimed that most of his behaviors stemmed from being placed in the wrong environment and that they were a method of escape when he couldn't complete the work that was given to him.

She taught me so much about effective teaching and really focused on Jamie's reading skills. She started from scratch with basic phonics. Jamie learned all of the sounds as we diligently worked with flash cards. We were finally getting somewhere.

She also targeted bad behaviors. It was an absolute nightmare to go anywhere in public with Jamie as he was now targeting people who wore glasses annoyingly singing, "Four eyes, four eyes, you need glasses to see." He also teased people in wheelchairs, laughing hysterically as he would repeat, "You broke your neck." He would also ask people (in potty terms) if they had passed gas if he smelled something bad. He was most often inappropriate when we were out in public. Whether it was a sensory issue, a learned behavior, or both—he had to stop.

Julie went on many outings with Jamie and me. She had a plan intact, and he seemed to listen to her. He knew she would take the time to enforce consequences for unwarranted behavior. Unfortunately, my disciplinary measures had been lacking for some time, and he had learned to get away with a lot. I always had three to keep up with when we were out in public and felt grateful and relieved most of the time when I didn't lose anyone. Though I tried very hard to be consistent and methodical, I failed miserably most of the time. At this point, I didn't know what else to do. I felt defeated. His behaviors were so prevalent, such an ongoing battle that I just couldn't punish, fuss, or scold any longer. I was so grateful for her help.

Within about two months, Jamie was calm and quite cooperative. He really enjoyed the quiet and relaxed environment at home. He was really trying. I remember him faithfully working on an online spelling website that I had subscribed to in the afternoons so that I could shower and dress. He never failed to adhere to his schedule, and he continuously tried with all of his might. He was sweet, compliant, and even helped with household chores. After schoolwork in the afternoon, he would cheerfully sing church hymns and Ray Charles tunes as I accompanied him on the piano. We called this "music class."

With Julie's help, he was on the right track and was definitely making progress in reading and spelling. I had even taught him subtraction. He had only known his addition facts when I brought him home. After much failure in trying to teach him to subtract, I finally began to teach it as "undoing addition." Instead of saying what is nine minus six, I would say six plus what equals nine. It worked like a charm. Soon he had all of his subtraction facts mastered. He was certainly capable of learning. I just needed the right approach.

I was so amazed with his progress and really began to enjoy our days together as they were so productive. I felt like I was bonding with my child all over again. I was able to give him the adequate attention and affection he needed. It was a blessing to have a positive, life-giving relationship with my child. I no longer had to run around like a chicken with my head cut off putting out fires between the three. This alone time with him gave me the opportunity to be patient, gentle, and tuned in to his needs. Once the other two were home from school, Jamie was able to relax and play. There was no more angst or attention-seeking behaviors. There was no longer a need to act up in order to escape hard tasks. He had been given the most loving attention throughout the day and was beginning to feel good about himself and all of his accomplishments.

During the six months Julie worked with Jamie, she continued to voice strong feelings about his return to school in a mainstream classroom in the fall. She felt this was of utmost importance for his socialization and overall well-being. Her main goal was to get him classroom ready. She emphatically stressed the importance and the value of the school setting. She influenced me to start shopping and even visited a few schools with me. She would take great care to interview the teachers and principals, making sure Jamie was placed in the right environment.

In the meantime, I had put all three of my children's name on a waiting list for an incredible charter school that was opening the doors in the fall. It was geared towards a classical education, rich in history, art, and literature. As I found myself becoming disgruntled with the trends in education in general, I found this to be an extraordinary opportunity. I never dreamed that they would get in.

As some of the last names on the waiting list, luck would prevail, and all three children won a spot in the new school. It was a last-minute unexpected opportunity, and Julie was not able to interview the staff for me. However, I spoke with the principal before accepting and painted the picture of Jamie as the well-behaved homeschool student that he currently was. I explained that he had autism but would just need extra help with assignments. She assured me that Jamie would be assisted in the classroom as much as possible. I was encouraged and couldn't help wondering if this had been God's plan for Jamie all along.

As Julie and I discussed, there was no special education department yet set up in this brand-new school. We were almost thankful of this fact. We thought that if he was expected to function independently in the classroom then he would eventually succumb, and by necessity, learn exponentially. Because of this great hope, I was dragging my feet on getting his formal I.E.P (Individual Education Plan) to the administration. It obviously showed him functioning at a very low level. Honestly, we wanted to see what he could do aside from any preconceived notions.

I enrolled all three children with all the best intentions and hope in the world. Drew started first grade there, and as I held Jamie back in homeschool, I was able to start him in third grade with Lisbeth, though they would have different teachers.

It took two weeks for his teacher to confront me. He had had a few behavior hiccups in the first few days which we widely anticipated. The teacher seemed to be relaxed about it at the time. Really, there were no major altercations. It wasn't until she saw his IEP that she became incensed and sent him packing. She was angry and told me point blank that Jamie should have never been in her classroom. As I explained that I had spoken to the principal and was working with an A.B.A. therapist who insisted that he needed to be in the mainstream classroom, she had no sympathy.

The rest of the school faculty was kind and offered to provide services for him the best they could. This would entail him being in a small little office with a special education teacher all day. Jamie was heartbroken. He kept trying to tell me, "Mommy, I was good. I didn't do anything wrong. Why can't I go back?" I called Julie sobbing. She dropped what she was doing and immediately came over. She was furious and wanted to pay the teacher and principal a visit. The truth was: I had two other children at that school and they mattered as well. I wanted no bad feelings to follow them around. I told Julie that I would rather not fight it. I also did not want Jamie to be someplace he was not welcome. I guarded his heart very carefully. I could not and would not take the chance that someone would damage his little self-esteem.

It's always painful when you've done absolutely everything you can, tried your best, and sacrificed to the moon and back only to be kicked in the gut. This was how I felt. And I felt even worse for my little boy who wanted desperately to go to school and be accepted. It seemed there was no place for him.

## Houston, We Have a Problem

In the spring of 2011, Beau took a transfer to Houston, Texas. It was bittersweet because we loved our community dearly, but we couldn't help looking forward to being closer to our family. Our hometown of Lafayette was only a four-hour drive from Houston.

We were optimistic about the move. I had spoken at length to the principal of the neighborhood school the children would be attending. He assured me that Jamie would be placed in the regular classroom with plenty of support. I have to admit, I was very excited for this new beginning. I had hoped this school would provide Jamie the opportunity to learn and flourish.

It was March of 2011 when we moved into our new house in a beautiful community northwest of Houston. It was an easier move. The neighbors were very friendly. There were lots of kids, the school was close by, and our family embarked on a new adventure.

As the kids settled in school and I finally had everything put away and decorated, I found myself feeling lost without the chaos. I wasn't used to being home alone with no one but the dog to keep me company. I was missing the adrenaline rush of managing behaviors, schooling, therapy of every kind, cooking and cleaning frantically, as well as kids running around in and out of my house. But I eventually got over myself, joined a lady's bible study at our church, and started running.

Our family quickly settled in and adjusted beautifully at first. We were happy to be reunited with very close friends from our past. These were the greatest of friends that loved our family unconditionally. Being close to them and a short car ride away from our immediate families was definitely the highlight of our move.

But soon the phone started ringing. Jamie was having behavioral problems at school. He was being non-compliant with his schoolwork and relentlessly pestering the other children. At home, he and Drew were starting to fuss as well.

The school work he was bringing home was definitely above his level. I would spend hours with him after school, but inwardly knew it was just too hard. They did not modify his work. I went from a school where he was counting pennies and dimes in an inclusive significant support to a school where he was just plopped into a regular classroom with all the expectations of the other kids. Though he had two resource classes where he did receive support during the day, he was still struggling with all of the material and concepts. So, my little son did what he always did when he felt stressed, he acted out. Before it was all over with, due to some very stern teachers, he was even labeled O.D.D. (Oppositional Defiant Disorder). I thought to myself, "Great! Another label!"

In efforts to help, Beau and I hired one of his sweetest resource teachers to tutor him every afternoon. She was truly amazing. She worked beautifully with him. He was completely compliant and worked very well with her. Between the tutoring, and my help with homework after school, I thought things would get better.

I also hired a behavioral specialist to accompany me to his IEP meeting. Here we would air out the problems trying to put in place interventions to help Jamie. This lady was an expert at the process and very knowledgeable, but it was really a waste of money.

I was becoming quite frustrated with the never-ending school battle, and my character was being shaped alright— into the shape of a pitchfork. My sarcastic, bitter insides were shouting during this meeting, "HEY YOU MORONS WITH ALL OF YOUR USELESS CREDENTIALS! JUST TEACH MY KID TO READ, WRITE, AND DO MATH. JUST BE PATIENT AND KIND WITH HIM. ALL YOU NEED IS A BOOK, PAPER AND PENCIL!" I was pretty fed up, but kept a smile on my face and wrote the four-hundred-dollar check for this advocacy service which bore absolutely no fruit. I was wearing down at this point. It seemed there was no help for him. It was so much simpler than school administrators made it out to be. I do believe his tutor, Jana, was on the right track and making progress with him. I thought, "If he just had her all-day long." Then I began to think outside of the box.

I was shot down immediately by Beau when I mentioned homeschooling again. He was adamant that Jamie needed to be in a social environment. But it seemed like nothing was working and everything was just getting worse. Relations in the neighborhood were also going south.

I was mortified that my sweet precious boy who had overcome so many behavioral issues was regressing. Of course, I understood very well that the stress of the move could play a part. I knew he needed an adjustment period, but his behavior continually got worse despite every effort on my part.

The kids in our new neighborhood, though they were good kids, were not quite as tolerant as the kids back home in Denver. No one even gave him a chance, and he was ostracized immediately. He was never included. Of course, this meant one thing—his behaviors got exponentially worse.

As Jamie got older, I found that people were less sympathetic and compassionate. He wasn't little anymore, and behaviors were rarely excused.

He was putting red ants down the mean girl's shirt, shouting bad words, grabbing things from people and running away. Once, a neighbor came to my door holding Jamie by the arm. It turns out that Jamie and the neighbor's son were grappling over a lizard. The man was quivering, and his voice was shaking as he tried not to shout. He angrily explained what happened, revealing that in the process the poor lizard's tail came off.

This was not one of my best moments I will admit as I replied, "Look man, Jamie has autism and I'm very sorry he behaved that way. It is hard to contain him in the house. I am very protective of him and try to keep an eye on him, but he is a ten-year-old little boy." I calmly continued, "In fact, I begged my husband to move us to the country where Jamie would be free to roam without offending others, but he couldn't commute that far. And by the way, if you live in the south you should know that a lizard's tail grows back."

The man was shaken to his core. He did not know Jamie had autism. Like everyone else, he assumed Jamie was a product of poor parenting. It was obvious that he felt horrible after the fact and immediately started apologizing and inviting us to dinner. I just said, "Sure, we will think about it." Time after time this man would extend the invitation over the next year, but Beau declined. This was a nice family, and I handled this poorly. At this time, however, I don't think I was even capable of understanding his point of view. I was getting pretty "done" with people, and that's such a bad way to be.

As a result of all of his neighborhood shenanigans, I kept Jamie with me inside or in the backyard. He was allowed to play with Drew and his friends in the backyard, but they always ended up fighting. A real unpleasant season began between the brothers that year. Drew became angry and resentful, and Jamie's emotions were out of control.

Jamie was also teasing children on the school bus. After many warnings, I refused to let him get on one morning. I would drive him to school as long as he was teasing. This greatly upset him. He had a real problem with being separated from the typical kids. He was starting to understand that he was different and didn't like it one bit.

As I turned around to put him in the car after the other two left on the bus, I could not find Jamie. I searched the house and eventually saw that his bike was gone. I started off in my van looking for him and soon became hysterical when the school phoned me on my cell. The kids on the bus alerted the driver when they saw Jamie riding behind on his bike. The problem was that the bus was on a six-lane divided highway now, and Jamie was on it too. Worried sick, I tried to catch up. Luckily, the vice principal was phoned as she was passing by. She stopped him on the highway, put his bike in her car and drove him to school. I was sobbing endlessly when I got there. He could have easily been killed.

I remember asking Jamie later how he managed to cross the busy street. He told me there was a nice policeman who assisted him to the other side. This had me baffled. This was a six-lane road separated by a median. There were no bikes on this street and no crosswalks. Furthermore, I had never seen a police car stopped anywhere in the vicinity aiming to help people, much less a vulnerable ten-year-old on a bike cross this busy road. It didn't make sense. My son had never been untruthful nor had he a history of exaggerating. He was pretty much incapable of doing so. Beau and I wholeheartedly believed him and looked at each other with smiles and raised eyebrows as to convey, "Are you thinking what I'm thinking?" We still wonder, to this very day, if he was protected supernaturally.

The principal and all involved were ultra-kind and helpful. They arranged for a special bus with a monitor to pick him up from that day forward. This proved to be such a blessing. The bus driver and monitor were the sweetest ladies in the world. They were friendly with me and just loved Jamie to death. They always complimented him telling him how cute, well-dressed, polite, and sweet he was. He enjoyed riding the bus, and I loved getting to visit with my nice friends. They always brightened my day. It was like they came from an alternate universe. I wasn't used to people being so nice, not even the ladies in my Bible study. I knew God had his hand in this all the way.

Still, I found myself in a bad way as a negative spirit rose up within me. Amongst all of the nice neighbors that we had, I dwelt on the cranky one who fussed at me for everything, hurting my feelings many times over all of my children. I couldn't get over it enough to appreciate wonderful Joe next door, Steve down the street, Lana, my wonderful backyard neighbor, the Landrys, the Masons, the Salazars, and many others that extended so much kindness to our family. There was a lot going on. The pressure was starting to mount, and I was obviously starting to buckle. I think I was just tired of everything being so hard.

My darling Lisbeth was starting to have some problems of her own. She was having a very hard time in school. She was now in the same grade with Jamie for the first time and feeling all kinds of social pressure. Foremost, she was being teased and bullied. She was also having a hard time with the tricky common core math they were implementing. And on top of everything, her fourth-grade teacher was unkind, humiliated her, and basically told me Lisbeth had A.D.D. (Attention Deficit Disorder) when I conferenced with her.

My poor little girl eventually got to where she would not come out of her room. Lisbeth was always so social and full of life. Now withdrawn into a life of computer games, she stayed inside. I tried and tried to facilitate play dates. I also coaxed her into playing volleyball where the little girls were unaccepting to say the least, and the coach was no nicer. I had sleepovers and parties for her. She would willingly participate, but never initiated any sort of social endeavor on her own. I also tried giving her time to adjust. I figured she might need her space without being judged or prodded. She lovingly and happily participated in the family but preferred to stay inside and never desired any sort of social interaction. After a while, I was concerned because I could see this was a definite change. She simultaneously started having severe stomach problems. I took her to several doctors and gastroenterologists in Houston's medical city. There was no diagnosis. She ended up with x-rays and an over the counter laxative.

She finally admitted all of the problems at school, the social stigma she felt from Jamie and the fact that she missed "home." She appeared depressed. I slept with her, holding her many nights as she cried. I was insanely worried about my sad little girl. It seemed like there was nothing I could do to help. All I could do was love her and spend time with her, so that's what I did.

There were so many good things about moving to Houston and so many good people in our midst, but it seemed like everything was just getting worse for everyone. Beau's commute was about three hours total each day—and that was when he was home. He traveled two weeks out of every month. He hated that part of his job. We were both so lonely when we were apart. Looking back now, I regret blaming everything on the move.

We had still had problems when we lived in Denver, but we were happy. It didn't seem like anyone was happy anymore. It was so hot outside that summer, you rarely saw kids playing outside. I came to understand why everyone and their brother had a swimming pool.

But there were good times too. In lieu of a swimming pool one hot morning, Drew and I dug a really cool pond. We fixed it up with a water pump waterfall, a beautiful lily pad and some pretty fish. It ended up looking really nice, and he enjoyed searching for turtles and frogs to put in it.

Our family will always have special memories of the wonderful weekend we spent at the Mason's river house where the kids were able to hydro slide and waterski. We also had a memorable surprise birthday party for Beau with our closest friends, and were blessed with the opportunity to connect with our sweet family members in Dallas that year. Though trouble reared its ugly head from time to time, we did have joy and so much to be thankful for, but the elephant in the room was we all wanted to move back to Denver. Beau and I both felt deeply that Denver was our home.

As this was ridiculously discussed less than one year after we moved, we decided to pray about it fervently. This was a very big decision. In order to make this happen, he would have to quit his job where he was making more money than he ever had, and find a new job in Denver. We would have to sell our new home for a loss, move ourselves back (a very costly venture in itself), find a new home, and basically start all over again. This could not be a rash decision, so we prayed. We actually asked the Lord point blank if we should move back.

After Christmas, we revisited the idea of moving back to Denver. I can admit, as badly as I wanted to move back, I asked God to control the situation according to His will, and He answered. We both felt after praying, it was the right thing to do.

In March of 2012 we stuck a for sale sign in our yard and moved back to Highlands Ranch. Yes, the Lord had provided Beau with a brand-new job with a great company that provided for our entire move. We hadn't sold our house yet, therefore, we were moving into an apartment in the school zone where we needed to be. I followed Jamie's beloved para-professional, Miss G., to a neighboring school. This school had an excellent reputation and though in a different school zone, was very close to our old home. Miss G. thought highly of the S.P.E.D. (Special Education Department) there and recommended that I register all the children there as it would be convenient, so I did.

We loved life in the apartment. It was so easy, fun, and scaled back. I was happy to say, "less is definitely more." We backed up to one of the most beautiful bike trails in Denver. We all rode bikes together, swam, relaxed and connected with many old friends. Everyone was happy and glad to be back. Lisbeth was coming around again and seemed to be getting back to normal. School was going well for all including Jamie who was adjusting nicely in the care of Miss G. and the kind special needs director.

Our house in Houston sold quickly, and we were able to purchase a home in the new school zone. We moved in our new home in June of that year. The kids became reacquainted with old friends and met many new ones. Beau loved his job, and I couldn't have been happier and more grateful.

I will never regret that year in Houston. As we all look back now we tend to remember only the good stuff. I choose to remember our very special friends and family that blessed our time there. I continue to believe that God had a special plan for us to be there that particular year.

During the one year we lived in Houston, my dear mother was diagnosed with breast cancer. Through good times and bad, she had always been there for me. She nurtured and cared for us all with a loving heart and the spirit of a servant. I was so grateful for the opportunity to be there for her through surgery and recovery.

Also, Beau's dad, due to a mild heart attack, was sentenced to his third coronary artery bypass surgery. Few people live long enough to have three of these surgeries, and it is not a common occurrence by any means. It was definitely serious business, and I was well aware of this. We were extremely concerned but were able to be there through the worst of it due to proximity. It was a blessing and a gift to be there for our family during these very critical times. Perhaps it was part of God's plan for us to be there for that one year to support our beloved parents who had always been there for us.

What I learned is that in everything, there is always "both." There is both joy and sadness. There are always both kind people and insensitive ones. There are always good times and bad, laughter and tears, triumphs and troubles. We must live to accept the both in everything.

Time and time again the enemy persuades me to meditate on the bad things, the mean-spirited people, the hurts, and the frustrations. This year in Houston helped me to recognize this. The Holy Spirit leads me to believe that the only way to release the bad stuff is to admit it, accept it, and then move on. It is then that we are free to go about our business relishing the good and living in gratitude. The truth is that God actually blessed us in many ways during our one year in Houston, and our family will always have very fond memories.

## Chapter Four
# Hidden Blessings

*"Come Thou Fount of every blessing, teach my heart to sing Thy grace, Streams of mercy, never ceasing, Call for songs of loudest praise."*

— *"Come Thou Fount of every blessing,"*
*Robert Robinson (1757)*

We were very grateful to be back in our old community, in our new house, and in a new school. Though our family seemed to be happy and thriving, I found the later elementary years trying my patience and wearing me down but also changing me, creating in me a whole new perspective of parenting.

Parenting a child with autism who cannot control his emotions and keeping the peace between the other two siblings was quite challenging to say the least. These were the years where I felt there was constant strife in the household. There was bickering, name calling, and the startling sound of slamming doors. They fought over cookies, TV programs, and friends. It seemed that there was always contention.

Jamie was not faring well in this environment. He could be set off into a tailspin quicker by his siblings than any other force in his life. For Lisbeth and Drew, the time had come. They were getting frustrated with his embarrassing behavior around the neighborhood and at school. They were also tired of him repeating weird catchphrases. It seemed he would do anything to get a rise out of them. Jamie's emotional outbursts were causing a calamity in the household every single day, and everyone suffered because of it.

We were also still at the point where going out in public with him was a real punishment. Truly, we stayed to ourselves as much as we could out of self-preservation. We had been there and done that. We didn't fare well altogether in society.

I believe Lisbeth faced the most ridicule and embarrassment as they were in the same grade. Though they were in different classes, she was always having to answer to his behavior. She even stopped inviting friends over to spend the night because Jamie would follow them around asking them if they wanted to "make out." Yes, I dealt with him over and over, lecturing and enforcing consequences, but Lisbeth was developing a deep resentment for Jamie.

My tactics had to change for Jamie's sake as well as Lisbeth and Drew. There was too much fussing on my part and too much resentment on theirs. I loved them all way too much to be constantly correcting and wanted more than anything to have a peaceful, loving, home. In order to make this happen, love and compassion had to prevail, and it started with Jamie. We had all been given a big assignment. Beau would continually remind the other two that God gave Jamie to all of us.

As I prayed for God's guidance on this, I was led to a book called "Shepherding a Child's Heart" by Ted Tripp.[1] This was a life-changing read that blessed our family by changing my perspective. It teaches that behavior is a matter of the heart. My entire goal had to be about creating a desire for obedience in my children's heart. It is by knowing the true nature of God and the love that Jesus displayed by dying in our place, that our hearts can be transformed.

This profound concept really changed my perspective on parenting. I started focusing on the fruits of the Spirit: love, joy, peace, patience, kindness, goodness, faithfulness, gentleness and self-control. This book helped me to understand that within the heart lies the root of all behavior. The goal is to cultivate a Godly heart and attitude. It was a totally different approach. It allowed me to parent in a more meaningful manner, avoiding the pitfall of reward and punishment.

I started to see some positive changes within my children and also in myself. I became less frustrated and less grumpy. Certainly no one deserved a gold medal for behavior in my home, but things were definitely getting better.

Beau was really effective at explaining scripture to the children and applying it to our family situation. He would quote Luke 12:48 which says, "From everyone who has been given much, much will be demanded and from the one who has been entrusted with much, much more will be asked." He explained to Lisbeth and Drew that they had been gifted with many talents and that this scripture points out that they are expected by God to use those talents to not only serve themselves but to serve God by helping others. They had many opportunities to teach Jamie and help Jamie along socially.

As his peers, their influence on him was much stronger than ours. Instead of getting frustrated and mad at him, they could turn the most annoying situations into a teaching moment. Drew really took to this and really started helping us out.

I noticed Drew coaching Jamie on responses to conversation. He would also instruct him on proper body language. He would rightfully teach Jamie to not get too close to people when asking a question, but instead, put a little personal space between them. These were things I had been working on with Jamie, it seemed forever, but Drew was reaching him right away.

Yes, we were teaching Lisbeth and Drew to help Jamie along, but more importantly, we were teaching them to love him and have patience with him as this was pleasing to the Lord. In time, and after much prayer, it seemed their hearts changed, and a little more love and compassion permeated our home.

We tried to do many fun things together as a family in efforts to bring our family unit back together. Beau even bought a camper thinking it might bring us all closer, and it worked (team bonding, I guess you would call it). We enjoyed the simple things about camping together: a beautiful hike, fishing, roasting hot dogs and smores, and watching Mabel chase the ground squirrels. We shared many laughs and inside jokes so ridiculous that no one could possibly understand. Jamie was still so socially limited and so distant most of the time, but in this setting, he was calm. He was definitely happy and feeling loved.

This new approach to parenting was a blessing indeed and was totally effective with Lisbeth and Drew, but with Jamie, I needed something more. There was still much work to do preparing him for the integration into society. We continued to relentlessly work on behavior with him and also pressed on with activities and interventions that would expand his world.

Though behaviors were quite a burden for many years, there were many hidden blessings during this time that collectively made a big difference. Every positive experience and every special friendship brought Jamie closer to a functional life.

He and his brother were committed to a Taekwondo class for a year or so. This program was great. The instructors were very encouraging and helpful. They had expectations and did not allow slacking but promoted good attitudes and character development. It was a great atmosphere for Jamie, and I believe learning the forms and constantly obeying verbal commands really helped his auditory processing. It also boosted his self-esteem and gave him a little confidence.

He also attended *Sylvan* learning center for a period of about two years. There was not a lot of clear cut academic progress noted due to the fact that most of the work was independent work. Still, he learned to sit, listen, follow directions, and be compliant. The instructors were so incredibly nice and tolerant that he actually enjoyed it. He always behaved nicely here as they gave him lots of positive feedback. This made all the difference in the world. He was definitely gaining some ground socially.

And then something really big happened. When Jamie was in sixth grade, two of the nicest boys, Ethan and David, took him under their wing. They included him at school recess and even came over to our house to hang out with him on the weekends. I have the most endearing picture of them sandwiching him in the middle with their arms draped over him. The picture says it all. They guided, protected, and encouraged him along for years.

Even in sixth grade, Jamie had few interests and few things to talk about. He still routinely perseverated on things of the past. In spite of this, they were still happy to come over and hang out with him and even sleep over. They would jump on the trampoline with him, play video games, and teach him to play basketball. I believe he learned so much just being around them. There is no doubt in my mind that God was all about this. Every night, for many years, I had specifically prayed that Jamie would find a special friend. He got two, and they were absolutely the best boys you could ever meet.

However, sixth grade was still a tough year for him. I suppose his hormones were changing, and he was dealing with a great deal of frustration. We had several holes to patch in the sheetrock in the basement to prove it. I believe that part of Jamie's emotional outbursts stemmed from the realization of how differently he was treated compared to the other boys at school.

We lived about a mile from the elementary school and enjoyed walking to and from school during the beautiful season (from May to October). During this final year of elementary school, he started begging to ride his bike to school independently. This meant so much to him because many of his friends did. I believe he was counting on it being the one thing that would make him feel a little normal as he was still chaperoned by special needs teachers all day long. I was encouraged that he had the self-awareness to care.

I had, for many years, ridden bikes with him teaching him to wear a helmet and to look both ways when he crossed the street. I knew I had to let him go. It caused me great anxiety to let him ride away from me independently, even though I was close by walking with the others. But I had to let him go. I received a lot of disgruntled looks and comments from some teachers who acted like I had lost my mind. Nevertheless, I was used to being judged and ridiculed by now and let my precious boy do what he desperately needed to do.

This independence, riding his bike, was wonderful for him. It was exactly what he needed. He was so proud and started trying much harder to emulate the other boys. His behaviors actually improved. He appreciated the confidence I had in him and made sure to never let me down.

Beau and I started realizing how important it was for Jamie to have a typical life. It was his heart's desire. He wanted to be treated like a regular kid and despised any special treatment that would set him apart. In light of this, we began to give him chores and responsibilities. Beau taught him to mow the grass, and I was teaching him about dishes, trash duties, and bathing the dog. He would help me vacuum out my car, clean out the garage, and rake the leaves. Though his attention span was about fifteen to twenty minutes, he was so sweet and proud to help.

We realized how desperately Jamie yearned to be like every other kid. He wanted to be in the classroom and work independently. He wanted to go to birthday parties, sleepovers, and Sunday school without Mom holding his hand or at least peaking around the corner with bated breath. Beau and I desperately wanted this for him as well. But none of this was possible as long as Jamie was still saying inappropriate things. I even toyed with the idea that he might have Tourette's syndrome and could not help it, but I knew that was not the case. The fact was that this was an area beyond my control. I could not roll up my sleeves and make him behave. Surely, this was a job for someone infinitely greater than I.

*Chapter Five*

# A New Approach

*"But they who hope in the Lord will renew their strength, they will soar on wings like eagles, they will run and not be weary: they will walk and not be faint."*

—Isaiah 40:31

Jamie's very special speech therapist explained to me years ago that autism has layers: language and communication, auditory processing, sensory integration, and socialization to name a few. She said that you just have to keep peeling.

I came to realize that his behaviors might be one of the hardest layers to peel. At this time, he would still shout out inappropriate things, say naughty words, and laugh when people would become upset. He would even tease the children in his special needs classroom at school. We knew it was functional for him out of anxiety, attention, or for escape, but we couldn't seem to squelch it. This behavior was the number one barrier between him and the life that he claimed he wanted. We counseled him and prayed with him at length. It just seemed like this layer was stuck.

Jamie's behaviors were such an intense burden to our family for such a long time. I would say from second to sixth grade, we had all been truly tormented. I did not know what to do. I could not always isolate him. In fact, I would not isolate him from society. I just kept on giving him chance after chance. I knew he was not a monster. I knew that somehow, he had to learn self-control and etiquette in public. He was, deep inside, this precious child longing to be heard and accepted. Though I tried to encourage and inspire him with positive affirmations and love every single day, my efforts usually failed. I always started out in a positive light, but I ended up in the same old cycle of negative reinforcement. I reprimanded him, enforced consequences, counseled him at length, and many times lost my patience. I spent countless hours praying over him and with him.

By the end of Jamie's sixth grade year Beau and I were at our wits end. We had employed the help of many behavioral therapists. I also had him in social groups. My sweet mother even tried to help by teaching Jamie a special prayer to say at the onset of any bad words. It did help some, and we all reminded him to say it, including some of the teachers at school. At home, I was constantly modeling appropriate conversation, giving him topics to talk about and would role play with him. I would also brush him using the Wilbarger protocol and use social stories before any social situation. I felt endless compassion for him.

Beau and I were raised by hard-working, no nonsense parents. They were loving and kind, but there was no sticker chart on the wall with smiley faces for good behavior. We were both expected to be polite, respectful, tell the truth and obey our parents. Good behavior was an expectation, and there was no reward for it. All we knew were very unpleasant consequences if we failed. Our parents were definitely not afraid to use corporal punishment. Beau and I thoughtfully tried that too, but neither of us felt like it was appropriate or effective. We would never be at peace with spanking him. We prayed about it and decided that of all the interventions, we could not bear this burden.

This was all we knew about discipline. The parent handbook we received when Jamie was born left out the chapter about dealing with obnoxious, obscene, ruthless, and incorrigible behavior.

But we loved our child with a passion and had no problem changing our methods to try to help him. We did everything under the sun to discipline him effectively. I had faithfully instituted behavior charts with stars, rewards on slips of paper to be awarded upon good behavior and kept logs to identify triggers. I also begged, pleaded, and promised him the moon. We tried to keep it positive, but sometimes it was just impossible. He never responded very well.

The special needs room teachers at his elementary school did a great job keeping his behaviors under control, but this was to his detriment. They had to keep him in a controlled environment to contain these behaviors. What he really needed was to be mainstreamed with kids that he could model and learn from. Instead he was confined to a room with significant needs children who possessed very little language and almost non-existent social skills.

I had to have a plan at home — a different plan. I was constantly reading and researching behaviors, mostly from the Christian viewpoint. I also prayed incessantly for God to reveal to us, as

I AM THE CLAY

parents, how to love our child and discipline him at the same time. The answer did come, and it was pretty radical.

I had joined a bible study at our church, and one day went out to lunch with the ladies. I was normally reluctant to socialize because I had nothing to visit about except the nightmare my family and I were experiencing at home every day. Hearing about other people's normal, happy lives tended to make me very sad (pitiful but true). I felt compelled to go and subsequently bonded with the sweet ladies.

One lady opened up about a troubled teen she had at home who had serious behavior problems. She finally found a counselor who gave her a completely different approach...and it worked. It was amazing to hear. It had to do with unconditional love. I digested every word she had to say and prayed about it all for a couple of weeks. I was finally blessed with a plan. I had no hesitation. There was no turning back. God opened my mind and heart. I knew the plan was His. I was no longer in control and finally felt a sense of freedom.

God placed it upon my heart to refrain from disciplining him for any behavior outburst. Mercy would rule, and there would be absolutely no consequences for anything. I was to hug him each time he acted up telling him how much I love him. I would then affirm that God made him wonderful. After much love and encouragement, I would gently tell him that he would never have the life he wanted if he kept behaving this way. I would tell him how important his life was and how special he was in God's eyes. I would show him a lot of scripture confirming his identity in Christ and how God had uniquely planned his personality. I would continue to tell him that if he chose to act this way, I would still love him. I would love him no matter what he said or did, and so would God.

This approach was geared at showing him the intense, unconditional, and everlasting love Jesus has for him. And as his parents, we loved him the same way. I made sure to contrast our love with Jesus' love for him. I pointed out that Jesus' love for him is perfect and that our love for him is not because we are sinners. I asked him for forgiveness for anytime we might have hurt his feelings in the past and assured him that God would never let him down.

It was a bit of a rocky road for a while as he tested all the boundaries he could. Most of the time I would ignore the bad words as though I didn't hear them and just say, "I love you my wonderful Jamie." It was almost comical how this rocked his world. He was truly speechless and looked like a deer in the headlights.

The other two children were none too happy. They thought he was getting a free pass to commit murder. We tried to explain it to them in confidence and asked them to follow suit. They were a little obstinate. Things were messy, but we got through it.

We continued to find reasons to praise him. He eventually became very motivated by the praise. He relished it and lived for it. It was obvious that he started to view himself as a valuable member of the family— a view he would never again let go of.

This was the turning point in his life. God had blessed us with a breakthrough. He began to change, morphed by unconditional love.

To me, accepting Christ's amazing grace and unconditional love compels me to do everything in my power to honor it. Out of a supernatural place I want to reciprocate. It drives my entire being. I don't want to let my heavenly Father down who loves me so much. By its nature, Grace is reciprocal—not earned but cherished. I was hoping that Jamie would respond the same way.

I prayed that Jamie would come to understand this very powerful truth. It was a matter of the heart. And he certainly did. He gobbled it up and slowly began to live to please God, his parents, his teachers, and his friends.

During the time that we implemented the unconditional love approach with Jamie, God placed it upon my heart to homeschool him. It was determined that I would homeschool Jamie during middle school.

He was indeed homeschooled during seventh and eighth grade and made remarkable gains. Jamie's life began to change. We really started seeing evidence of this profound change during these junior high years. For the first time, we saw him calm and cooperative during Sunday School at church. This was a huge breakthrough.

He had a history of acting up in Sunday School. For years, I volunteered in his classroom to help him. Once he entered fifth grade, he absolutely refused to let me accompany him. Holding my breath, I finally allowed him to go alone. I kept in tight communication with the director and sat in the main church service with a knot in my stomach the whole time. Every single Sunday, there was some sort of incident, either shouting out, accusing someone of farting, teasing, or simply laughing hysterically during small group. We disciplined him the best we could. Thankfully, the director and young teacher were very tolerant and kept welcoming him. I feel because of their patience, he eventually simmered down. His behavior was always markedly better with calm, kind, and accepting people.

During seventh grade, the Sunday School teacher approached me to report how polite and respectful Jamie had become. I'll never forget that day as long as I live. It was the first real glimmer of hope I ever felt for my son.

By the end of eighth grade, Jamie was a completely different boy. He had transformed into this fine young man. He had a cheerful attitude, offered to help with household chores, had excellent hygiene habits, and went to bed on schedule without being told. He made sure he ate a healthy diet avoiding junk food. He also had impeccable manners at home and in public. He would now ride his bike to the rec. center close to our home where he would run, swim, or play basketball with friends. He was finally starting to have a life. Although his mannerisms and conversation could still be a little awkward, his respectful and polite attitude carried him a very long way.

Today, he is the most gracious and loving young man. He never fails to tell me he loves me or give me a hug, even around peers. He is also very appreciative of anything you do for him. Amazingly, Jamie has also learned to be flexible and handles the answer "no" like a trooper.

Though I would love to say that he is beyond reproach, he still has issues from time to time. He still occasionally mutters inappropriate words under his breath in response to uncomfortable situations. I understand this is a response to his anxiety level; however, I still correct him and remind him to say his little prayer as his grandmother implemented long ago. It always works.

These changes in Jamie's behavior were nothing short of a miracle, and I thank the Lord every day for rescuing my son as well as my family from this hardship. My precious son would now be capable of having the life he so desired.

*Chapter Six*
# Education: The Lifeline

*"Oh Lord my God, when I in awesome wonder, consider all the worlds Thy hands have made, I see the stars, I hear the rolling thunder, The power throughout the universe displayed, Then sings my soul my Savior, God, to Thee, How great Thou art, How great Thou art"*

— *"How Great Thou Art," Stuart K. Hine and Carl Boberg (1885)*

By nature, I am a giver. I love giving my time, my energy, and my love to everyone. I enjoy cooking for people going through an illness. I enjoy baking for others in times of celebration. I enjoy cleaning, helping, and nurturing hearts. This is probably the reason I became a nurse. Helping others sincerely brings me joy. It's what I do to keep my spirits up. And as much as serving has delighted my soul, nothing could compare to the satisfaction I have received from teaching.

Though kind deeds are certainly appreciated— the food gets eaten, the dishes get dirty again, and hearts will never cease to become broken; however, something learned is a treasure forever. Teaching has become one of the greatest joys of my lifetime.

About ten years ago, I fell into teaching piano as some of the neighborhood kids knew I was a pianist and were asking for lessons. I adored the children and haphazardly begin to teach. I had absolutely no idea how much I would enjoy it.

I actually began my college career as a piano performance major on full scholarship at L.S.U. Though I made the career switch to nursing, I continued studying piano formally with the finest instructors for many years. I found that I had so much knowledge to share. I couldn't understand why I had never before had the desire to teach. But as my little students would faithfully practice and progress, I was hooked. It was finally something I could give that would last, and I fell in love with teaching.

Once my children entered into elementary school, their education became strikingly important to me. My teaching skills expanded to the academic world. When helping my children with homework, I was always able to help them learn the lessons more efficiently by merely simplifying them.

As the work became overcomplicated and irrelevant, I felt great voids in the public-school education my children were receiving. I eventually homeschooled all three of my children at different times and for various reasons. It was a highly successful venture as they all eventually returned to school with competence and confidence. Teaching my children and watching them delight in their own success has definitely been one of the highlights of my life.

# Honoring God Through Education

Reminding myself that I have no greater purpose than to serve my living God, I realized that educating our children is a prime way to honor and fulfill His purpose. I often would tell my children as I would drop them off at elementary school, "Work hard as though you are..." and they would cheerfully answer, "working for the Lord." (taken from Colossians 3:23 which reads, "Whatever you do, work at it with all your heart, as working for the Lord, not human masters.") I wanted them to understand that their goal was not to please their parents or their teachers, but through all of their efforts, to please and honor the Lord.

When I began homeschooling, I was well aware of the fact that I was not a trained teacher. I hung my hat on the fact that I could pray to God for the wisdom I needed. I thought that perhaps a more realistic and practical presentation of education might spark their interests and revitalize their spirit. I wanted my children to have a different kind of education, one that surpassed regular mundane learning. I wanted them to feel inspired and see the significance and relevance of everything. As I dove in head first without warning, I began to see the mysteries of God. I saw the Creator in everything. I saw no greater proof of God's existence than when I started teaching. I found Him there, in every element of life; therefore, I conclude that we draw nearer to Him when we learn.

I see Him in math, the way all numbers relate to each other and how all rational equations can be solved using these relationships and principals. I see Him in great literature. What a miracle that man can use the pen to convey such deep and powerful emotion explaining the complicated conditions of the human heart. I certainly see Him in science. He is the Creator of the intricate and unique life systems on earth. The delicate ecological balance that has maintained for at least millions of years shows His magnitude and grandeur. The human body is a miracle in itself, and through understanding it's perfect balance and design, I see the Author of Life. I definitely experience God with all of my senses through music. Music is truly a gift and a miracle of its own. In theory, the "circle of fifths" is phenomena that proves that music is always relational and rational. In short, music makes perfect sense, and as well as art, also serves to keep us balanced.

God is the focal part of every aspect of life. How can we educate our children vehemently denying this very foundation of truth? It would be a disjointed array of elaborate schemes and delusions of man's grandeur that produces nothing more than schizophrenic thinking. Have you visited public school lately? There are problems and I believe this is why. There is no foundation of truth.

# Barricades

In my opinion, one of the barricades to a formidable education seems to be ego— driving a profound humanistic belief that compels some educators to deny the existence of God. For the intelligentsia, they cannot get over their own intellect. The very brain brilliantly designed by God is what separates them from Him.

Unfortunately, what we have today is a small group of folks at the top of the education chain who don't have any contact with children, in charge of creating primary and secondary school curriculum and having complete autonomy over the content. And then there are those who, at their greatest point of impact, are teaching in the universities, unduly influencing the young minds, propagating their own views, and keeping their pupils as far away from the truth as possible.

I do not believe that one must be a believer in Christ in order to be educated properly. It is commonly known that a few founders of the Constitution of the United States were not believers. The Founding Fathers though they separated church from state, were careful not to separate God from state. They knew that the country would thrive only upon a foundation of Judeo-Christian principals.[1] Replacing these principals with ego-centric humanistic ideals has led to a great demise in education. Susan Schaeffer Macaulay remarks in her book *For the Children's Sake,* "The first task of education is a moral one, with the Judeo-Christian framework giving direction."[2] This is so very important that I can say that education is futile if there is no virtue.

An education based on trying to prove there is no God will lead to a wild unproductive goose chase. Here, the agenda becomes the problem. Our education system, as I see it, seems to be failing because political/social agenda has compromised the truth. Days are spent in primary schools not learning information but extrapolating from informational text. Environmental platforms, human rights, and race relations have become the topics of choice that seem to be more like an indoctrination rather than an education. There also seems to be much time spent on proving how wrong everything we have learned in the past about science and history has been. Education should never have an agenda other than serving the child and should never be based on opinion. The truth has certainly become subjective as information is obtained primarily online.

It is my observation that curriculum has been filled with manmade agenda—another barricade. To achieve this agenda, the educational elite must entirely remove the notion of God. He threatens their authority and power over the children's thoughts and attitudes. I truly do believe in freedom of religion. I also believe in the separation of church and state, but I do not believe that we have to throw God under the bus to achieve this. There need be no propagating Christianity, but at the same time there should not be any desperate counter attack of the belief system that our country was founded upon. Mentioning God's name does not rope and tie someone to a belief system against his or her will but only serves as a reminder of what freedoms we stand for in this country and why we have them. May we simply stick with the facts. Surely there can be no offense in that.

As a girl, growing up through elementary, middle, and high school, all of the information I received from my teachers was factual. I could not ever detect the slightest bias or political agenda. Back then, teachers were careful not to inject political party platforms in the history, civics or science lesson. It was unethical and skewed the truth. I miss those days. As I have witnessed, political, environmental, social justice platforms are at the focal point of education and supersede real learning today.

I have definitely seen this happen in my high schoolers' history as well as literature classes. Facts seem to be watered down with opinion. And though I am the proud owner of strong opinions on just about everything, I want my children to be taught the truth at all costs, whether it makes them uncomfortable or not. After all, it is from meditating on the facts that we form our own opinions. Each child should be valued enough to be allowed theirs.

Connor Boyack, in his thought-provoking book "Passion-Driven Education" refers to this practice of indoctrinating kids in the opinions and information decided arbitrarily for them as "authoritarianism."[3] He cautions parents to be concerned about the blind obedience created in an authoritarian style education. He makes the case, "Deference to authority permeates our society and has led to a submissive ignorant culture that bases opinion on what a few information brokers-elected officials, news reporters, etc. tell us about what we should worry. At worst, however, authoritarianism leads underdeveloped minds to unquestioningly embrace propaganda as truth."[4]

Along with ego and agenda, the death of the textbook, in my opinion, has affected education. Textbooks of the past were put through extensive reviews from some of the world's leading experts. A science book would be reviewed by some of the country's premiere scientists who have spent their life's work in the field. You would see many accolades, accomplishments, and many letters behind their names. Reviewing and contributing to a textbook was a process, a careful process to ensure that the students would be taught information that was accurate, absolute, and relevant to their learning. A textbook, to me, is a tried and true reference. What I have witnessed is that science in high school is primarily taught through power points obtained from a menagerie of web sites. In short, *Google* has become the new textbook, and that concerns me. I wholeheartedly believe that great care must be taken to thoughtfully plan out the important information we are teaching our children.

Once at a teacher conference with my daughter, I began to question the earth science teacher about her curriculum. I was wondering where we could go to find the course content. My daughter was not much of a note taker at the time, and I was really concerned that there was no textbook to reference. She answered that the textbook was outdated as it was fifteen years old and that Lisbeth should just "google" the subject matter that she was missing.

Well, as politely as I could be, I asked her, "This is earth science, right? How much has the earth changed in the past fifteen years?"

I was baffled and I'm sure it showed on my face. I also questioned her about the validity and integrity of the internet. I even went as far as to explain to her that I could write an article about boogers and put it on the internet. Surely, it would come up on the search engines. But who would know if I was the world's leading authority on boogers, or a five-year-old who had just picked my nose. I was trying to explain, in pitifully graphic detail, that information on the internet is unpredictable and unreliable.

The death of creativity is also on my list of problems. The "rubric" is a prime example of this. The rubric is a checklist of components that are to be included for the optimal grade. This is a common assessment tool in the federal common core education curriculum.[5] I believe this could be an asset for children if it included a general guideline and left room for creativity. The problem that I am seeing is that these rubrics call for a very specific criteria for writing pieces as well as art. By the time one of my children finishes a paper, according to these micromanaged criteria, there's not a creative thought left. What about a design class where the color, shape, dimension and pattern of the project is predetermined. Is that really considered art? I can clearly see why right-brained, creative kiddos struggle in school.

Another problem I see in this digital age of infinite information is how time-consuming and tedious technology can be. There are many barricades a student must break through in order to simply find all of the details to their assignment. There is internet access, usernames and passwords, visibility settings, as well as a menagerie of different websites, classroom websites, and even a specific site used for turning in their work. I have noticed this when helping my own children. Homework becomes a very frustrating scavenger hunt. I am not hating on technology in the classroom. I am just advocating for assignments to be easily accessible, concise, and in one place so that the majority of the student's time can be spent on the important work that lies within.

Lastly, the standardized testing has just gotten way out of control and way out of touch. I firmly believe that testing should only serve the needs of the student to reflect on knowledge gained as well as to diagnosis any gaps. It should never be a stipulation to a teacher's salary nor should it affect a school's funding. It's also very costly and time consuming. In my not so humble opinion, I see this as another huge barricade to education in the 21$^{st}$ century.

## "Your Child Has a Problem"

When my youngest son Drew was in fourth grade, he was having some trouble learning in school. The teachers were concerned, and Drew was verbalizing feelings of failure. I was actively volunteering in his classroom at the time. I knew him to be an avid reader and a deep thinker. I was quite puzzled. I met with his teachers on many occasions. They claimed he could not pay attention and that he was so far behind they were worried that it would be impossible for him to ever catch up. In addition to them all but diagnosing him with A.D.D. (Attention Deficit Disorder), the math teacher actually said, "I have never seen a child this behind in math before."

I knew that my son was dreamy, disorganized and distractible. This is his personality. He was a typical ten-year-old boy. I was very astute to spectrum disorders such as A.D.D. and never once considered that he had an attention problem. I inherently knew better. After some evaluation, I found that the school curriculum was extraordinarily stale and full of political agenda. It was geared towards micromanaging information, predominately on a global scale. There was very little high interest reading, instead boring informational text.

I also noted that the math curriculum was promoting "critical thinking" and "problem solving" skills to a new level. Much abstract thinking was required to solve these new age math concepts. Of course, I'm all in favor of critical thinking and problem solving, but I find it imperative that children master foundational skills before they are ready for this task. Is a fourth grader even capable of abstract thinking? Teaching math without the mastery of the facts and foundational properties of numbers is like telling a child to build a house with lumber and blueprint but lacking hammer and nails. The math curriculum used in Drew's school was designed to ultimately challenge our children, helping them soar to the top as brilliant mathematical minds. As much as I appreciate that, I also understand that a harder curriculum is not always a better one. You can design the most challenging curriculum known to man, but if the child fails to understand the methods, you have done absolutely nothing.

I noted the worksheets they were working on included reading pieces glorifying immigrant workers secretly planning a strike, hailing how helpful the unions were in this country. Much political agenda was woven in as a fine thread into this particular reading piece. It was unbelievable. And this is just one example. Also included in the curriculum were reading passages with controversial rhetoric instead of facts. Besides the fact that the piece I noticed was totally boring, I felt like these kids were being coerced into opinions instead of learning foundational information. I was not a happy camper.

I actually put the union/strike worksheet on *Facebook* to get the opinions of others. I didn't like the fact that the piece was politically charged. This was not an isolated incident as many worksheets like this one had come home. I was concerned about the trends in education and wanted some feedback. A good friend of mine who works for the *Dallas Morning News* newspaper saw my post and contacted me about the topic. Her colleague reported on many complaints and issues with the new Common Core Curriculum adopted by the U.S. Department of Education. He was doing a piece and wanted an interview. Of course, I said yes. I had a lot to say.

This nice gentleman arranged a scheduled phone interview. He had done his homework and had already been in contact with the publisher of the piece in question. I proceeded to explain how unhappy I was about the political agenda in the passage. He had a rebuttal from the publishing company ready. They argued that because this was a reading comprehension piece that content was not important. Well, let's just say my passionate Cajun heritage started showing itself, and my voice turned into a high-pitched squeal. I protested, "What do you mean content doesn't matter? These are ten-year-old children. What about an article promoting the benefits of smoking marijuana? Would we still claim content doesn't matter? It matters very much." I concluded by telling him that the time they spend on useless, insignificant, opinions robs the opportunity they have to teach these children some important concepts about the world. The reporter acknowledged my concern and paraphrased this point in the article.[6]

This was a scary moment for me, coming to the realization that our children's education is being designed and published by people who believe that content doesn't matter. After much deliberation and prayer, homeschooling seemed like a great option for Drew. He was definitely on board.

Many factors came into play regarding this decision. It was not one that I took lightly. The fact was that our family had made two major moves in one year. I felt it was possible that Drew could be behind or at least lack confidence due to the shuffling around and different curriculums he had been exposed to. It also became obvious to me that the teachers just wanted to label him A.D.D. and forget about it. The "interventions" they had implemented were failing. I did not see that anyone was going to great lengths to help him. I also saw that he was starting to feel bad about himself saying, "I'm just stupid that's all." This broke my heart in two. This would not stand.

Beau, in our previous discussions about homeschooling said, "absolutely not." He did not think it was a good idea. I know he was worried about my stress level. My nature is not calm, cool, and collected. I am hyper, passionate, and emotional. I am not, and will probably never be, the coveted woman mentioned in the book of Proverbs chapter 31, but I loved my son dearly and always had his best interests at heart.[7] Surely, I would do absolutely anything in the world to help him. I like to believe this was my best qualification for the job.

As I continued to pray about it, I asked God to change Beau's mind about the decision to homeschool if that was, in fact, what He wanted me to do. Incredibly, the next day I mentioned it to him, and he did not hesitate when he said yes. He jumped on board overnight. He did not even seem skeptical or reluctant. He appeared to have peace with the decision.

Drew and I began our homeschool journey after Christmas break 2014. I had absolutely no idea what I was doing, but I knew that whatever I would teach would be good. It was to be something he could build upon later. The plan was to give him some solid foundational tools, eventually sending him back to school when he was ready.

# First: A Philosophy of Education

I had read quite a bit about the Charlotte Mason style of education and was definitely a fan. Charlotte Mason was an educationalist in England who lived through the years 1842-1923.[8] She was an educator as well as a philosopher and a devout Christian. Her philosophy of education was to respect, love, and nurture the child showing them all of the delight and satisfaction learning had to offer. She was brilliant in her efforts to bring the children to a place where they loved learning. Here, the desire was none other than their own. She knew how to effectively motivate children, and as a result, she attained remarkable compliance and respect from them. She developed a very successful model of education which she taught in PNEU (Parents' National Education Union) schools. Her training was focused on first helping the children create good habits. Her famous quote which is the way she taught all of her students to think is: "I am, I can, I ought, I will."[9] She also held very valuable the skill of narration. She thought of it as the most important evaluation tool of all. Having a child tell in their own words what they have learned or read confirms comprehension far more accurate than any other method.[10]

She also cautioned educators strongly against "twaddle." She coined the term "twaddle" to convey useless, pointless information. She thought the content of a child's learning to be of utmost importance.[11]

She wrote several books, her last one being titled: *An Essay Towards a Philosophy of Education.* A current edition of *For the Children's Sake* by Susan Schaeffer Macaulay is available today where Charlotte Mason's philosophy and methods are explained in easy to relate to and practical examples.[12] This is the book that inspired all of my efforts and goals in homeschooling. With this philosophy, I would nurture my young son's entire being.

From the first day, I fell in love with homeschooling. With much direction from the Charlotte Mason website, I provided him with rich literature, history, and geography. We also worked on spelling, grammar, writing, and science. Most importantly, we did an hour and a half of math each day on the dry erase board. It became apparent that he was weak in his math facts, and this was greatly hindering his success. I stayed engaged with him four hours a day, and afterward, he worked on assignments independently for about an hour. The time flew. We were usually done by 1:30pm each day.

We started off the day reading the Bible. We then studied the American Revolution through fun facts, maps, and historical fiction. He learned U.S. geography including all the states and their capitals. As I allowed him to direct his own learning, he picked Africa next. He studied the countries and the culture with enthusiasm. We worked puzzles, checked out books, and watched documentaries from the library. When we got to Asia, we sang and danced to Bob Seger to learn the capital of Nepal.

In the relaxed atmosphere, Drew began to love reading again. He read many great novels, one right after the other—high interest books that he picked from my worthy list. His comprehension of the material was impressive. He was easily reading above his level. He filled out essay styled, in depth study guides and wrote many book reports. He read eagerly and wrote with much help. He rarely complained.

He certainly learned all of his math facts. I no longer left it up to him, as I saw to it. He regurgitated factors and multiples until he knew them by heart. At that point, it was a cinch to teach him fractions. Decimals and percentages came next. By the end of the school year, he had completely mastered these concepts. We continued on with some geometric formulas and measurements and eventually progressed to integers and solving for an unknown.

Drilling the facts, breaking each problem down into organized steps, and lots of perfect practice were the keys to his success. I loved seeing him gain confidence in math.

I concentrated on making math easy for him. That was my number one priority. Everything had to be easy. In order to make it easy, I broke it down into simple steps and worked every single problem with him until he could do it. The model I found helpful, taught to me by Jamie's masterful A.B.A. therapist Julie, was "I do," "We do," then "You do." This can only be done in a direct instruction setting, but boy does it work! The reward for all this time and effort was seeing his self-esteem soar and having him realize how capable he truly was.

The afternoons were designed for extracurricular fun. We often went to the rec. center and played racquet ball, basketball, or foosball. I eventually enrolled him in a homeschool P.E. class that he really enjoyed.

There were also many valuable unexpected learning opportunities. He went with me to the courthouse to plead down a traffic ticket. He also learned to bargain shop, calculate a 20% tip, and make homemade chocolate chip cookies. We went skiing most Fridays in the winter and planted beautiful flowers together in the spring. He learned so much from experiencing life.

My child did not have an attention disorder. As he was presented relevant and interesting information he became excited to learn. I had little trouble motivating him. He was wonderfully compliant and such a pleasure to teach. I took some great advice from Gloria (my valuable homeschool advisor) and had Drew tested before we started homeschool and again before he re-entered school. Guess what? My child who was "so very far behind" ended up "so very far ahead" after one year of homeschooling.

Seeing how homeschooling benefited Drew's mind body and soul, I couldn't wait to start Jamie the following year. Homeschooling Jamie through the middle school years was already planned and prevalent in my mind. I let him continue public school through sixth grade because he had friends and loved his teachers. Middle school would be different. He would be in a different building, with many different kids, different teachers, and most importantly — with different hormone levels. I knew this would be a golden opportunity to advance his reading skills with one-on-one interaction while sparing him the wrath of the cruelest kids in the world — junior high kids. I knew it would be a different ball game from here on out. His teachers in elementary school sheltered him from all ridicule and bullying. I doubted he would have the same fortune in seventh grade. Also, I was not so sure he would be mainstreamed at all. One thing I knew for certain was that it was imperative that he be in a classroom at least simulating learning, not in an isolated room simply managing the symptoms of his autism. I couldn't wait to see Jamie reap the benefits Drew had from homeschooling.

Drew and I had grown so close, and he learned so much during our time together homeschooling. There was no question that we would continue as fifth grade approached. I had spent the summer planning and organizing for two. I was excited to have both of the boys home and to teach a couple of classes together. I had such lofty goals and dreams.

I guess all good things must come to an end because it simply did not work out. Soon there was bickering and complaining. I thought I could squelch it with a little bit of fun as I printed out the words to Steve Winwood's bluesy "Roll with It" and had them memorize the words.[13] I would play the tune and enthusiastically sing with them. Yes, we sang and danced to this great tune on many occasions and even felt compelled to share it with Lisbeth a time or two. This song became our motto and a family favorite on road trips, but it didn't really solve the problem.

One day as I was nagging Drew once again to complete an assignment, I saw that we were done. His attitude had changed and homeschooling was no longer effective. It was no longer what he needed. Drew had always been extremely sociable, and as much as I hated to admit it, needed to return to school. As disgruntled as I had been with the public-school curriculum, I could no longer fill in the socialization gap. Kids like Drew are motivated by peers. Looking forward to spending time with friends, playing basketball at recess, or cracking jokes at lunch are the experiences that kids live for. Though I had enrolled him in a homeschool enrichment program, I can't deny I felt sad seeing him most days isolated in seat work. As hard as I tried to keep things fresh and fun, the truth was that Jamie needed all of my attention. Also, Drew was missing time with friends. Above all else, I valued the condition of my child's spirit. This would be the one brick wall I would bang my head upon more than once. I could never compete with the school experience. I came to realize that school has many unseen benefits.

There were two very important and prominent problems I encountered with homeschooling. One is the lack of healthy peer interaction through the day. Kids, when in a good environment at school, learn from their friends and are motivated by them. Secondly, the experiences children get from the variety of classes and teachers cannot be replicated at home with one teacher. Homeschooling is a lifestyle. Variety, peer interaction, as well as sports and leisure activities must be woven in. It takes years to create this perfect balance. It is definitely a challenge to create when homeschooling for a short emergency remediation stint.

However, a school is only as good as its teachers, and I found this to be a common denominator in a good education. If a school has apathetic teachers or an unhealthy environment, in my honest opinion, homeschooling is definitely the better option.

We switched Drew back into his original elementary school where he had attended kindergarten. All three of my children had gone through the primary grades there, and I knew the faculty to be outstanding. He knew most of the children as he had played baseball with them for several years. The atmosphere at this school tended to be more creative. He was blessed to have marvelous teachers who cared and inspired him to do his best. The switch proved very helpful. He enjoyed school again and had absolutely no problem with the material. He was a happy boy.

Yes, I went full circle with education, but in the end, I knew Drew would be fine. I like to think that we just "rolled with it." The brief respite gave him time to see how satisfying learning can be. It also gave him a taste of success that would motivate him and drive him a little bit further. I gave him all that I had for a solid year. It had to be enough because now, I had the enormous task of teaching Jamie. I would soon find out that education would, indeed, be Jamie's lifeline.

## Education as a Lifeline

There are no words that could possibly describe what a wonderful student Jamie was. Yes, he was this growing adolescent boy who could barely read or write, but truthfully, he was the world's best student. He had a willingness to learn I have never seen before. He was intent on being obedient in every circumstance. He never tried to escape work and never gave up no matter how difficult the material was.

His personality changed drastically from the year before. I feel as though it was because he was in a calm, quiet environment free from chaos and distraction— a safe, comfortable place. I also believe that he began to feel motivated as we started off talking about his great potential and his place in this world. Ironically, it was in this isolated and strange homeschool environment that I believe he started feeling like a typical kid for the first time. I did not have to control him, manipulate him, or bargain with him. There were no behavior charts at all. I just had to love him and teach him. He was held to the highest standard for once, and he ate it up. My child wanted for the first time. It was all I ever hoped for and needed in order to work with him. He wanted to learn, he wanted to be appropriate, and most of all he wanted to be accepted.

Interestingly enough, I might have been a part of a miracle greater than that. God completely transformed my heart, mind, and soul in order to be what Jamie needed the most. Through the experience of homeschooling, I had miraculously become the most patient, calm, encouraging, and positive person I know. I had prayed for God's help though. I prayed for this transformation because I knew I had to have a healthy spirit in order to help my son. I absolutely loved spending time with Jamie and helping him. It was, as it was teaching Drew, one of the highlights of my life.

## Fruit to Bear

What Jamie needed was not complicated. He did not need a PhD. or any highly skilled teacher. He simply needed to learn to read and comprehend at all costs. He needed to learn to write by formulating good sentences and using sound spelling. He also needed to learn basic arithmetic and to learn about the world through science and history.

Reading each day began with the Living Bible which paraphrased the content in easy to understand language. We began with the gospel of Matthew and read through the entire book, chapter by chapter. It was a great place to start as there was lots of action and interesting events including the greatest story of all—Jesus. Jamie loved it. We took turns reading paragraphs, and then I would have him narrate to me what he read. If he struggled, I always helped him.

My dear friend Julie had given me many pearls of wisdom regarding teaching reading. I also devoured Ronald Davis' book *The Gift of Dyslexia* as well as many reputable books regarding reading and visualization.[14] I did not feel inept. I felt empowered by what I learned from these insightful folks. The key was to have Jamie put a mental picture together with the words he was reading. For to merely sound out words using phonics was essentially useless. Reading always had to be for understanding.

I felt Jamie had profound dyslexia from the beginning. Though I am not qualified to make that evaluation, I figured I had nothing to lose by using the strategies. His reading could only improve, and it did.

I found enlarging the font, following the words with my finger, and using text in short left to right columns as well as highlighting the prepositions really helped. The prepositions were most troublesome because they had no visual, so I had to make a visual for each one by using prepositional phrases. "From" was forever being confused with "for," so I described a birthday gift he was to receive "from Gran." Likewise, I described a birthday gift that was intended "for Dad." We even described the gifts in detail so that he would be able to make a picture. We also used hand motions to show the action. This actually worked, and I did the same for other prepositions.

Reading began with short stories. We read each day for as long as he could last. I would take turns with him. It was very important not to let him get too tired. He had to read and process the information at the same time. This was extremely hard for him. Harder words I often read for him in the interest of not losing the comprehension piece. We stopped periodically in the story to assess what was going on. I had to make sure he was getting it. On many occasions he went blank. I would then fish for the information little by little and prompt him to retell it all together. I drew a lot of pictures for him and even acted out the scenes while reading.

We moved on from the readers to interesting easy-to-read novels. I tried to pick simple stories that would interest him. I found picking the right book made all the difference in the world. If it was no interest to him, it was a complete waste of time. Progressing from narration, I made written comprehension questions for him to answer independently after each chapter.

In constantly researching reading, I came upon a principal held by some that would influence the way I would prioritize reading. It is called the "Matthew Effect" named by psychologist Keith Stanovich who studied reading and language disabilities extensively.[15] The term comes from Matthew 25:29 (NIV) which says, "For whoever has will be given more, and they will have an abundance. Whoever does not have, even what they have will be taken from them." It is popularly summarized as "The rich get richer, and the poor get poorer." The idea is that if a child does not learn to read by third grade, his learning will exponentially diminish over time. Up until third grade a child is learning to read, but if it is not mastered by then, he/she will certainly fall further and further behind due to the fact that after third grade, children are now reading to learn. If the skill is not mastered with adequate proficiency, the child cannot continue to learn as his peers. I know in my heart this is what happened to Jamie.

ANNA GIDEON

By sixth grade, Jamie had failed to learn years of information. He had learned some things such as how to count money, tell time, and write a few sentences; but he was definitely getting "poorer" by the day. Although reading remained the biggest obstacle for learning, there was no doubt he was making progress. I only feared he could never progress enough to catch up to grade level. I finally had to succumb to my faith in God and just be thankful for the gains I was witnessing. But before I could totally let go, there was just one more thing.

Beau and I had been invited to a fund-raising chili dinner event hosted by my friend, Shannon. Shannon had started a Christian school in Rwanda which ministered to and educated the children as well as the entire community there. Our old neighbor and Beau's best friend Nick was managing the school and would speak about the children whose lives had been transformed by this school. We were thrilled to get to hear firsthand how God was specifically using our good friend, Nick, in restoring hope and dignity in this poor country. It was a special evening, and we were honored to be a part of something so anointed by God. Little did I know that God would also bless our family that night with some real help for our son.

During the course of the evening, I found myself talking to another friend from Bible study, Ann, who gave me the name of Jeffrey Freed. Her daughter who had long struggled in school was tutored by Jeffrey and had made significant gains. Ann's testimonial certainly had my attention. Mr. Freed, a credentialed educator for many years, had written a book called *Right- Brained Children in a Left -Brained World.*[16] According to Ann, he lived in Evergreen (about twenty miles away from our home) and was still tutoring kids. His specialty was helping kids visualize and memorize, relying on their creative, right-brained strengths.

Not letting any grass grow under my feet, I called Mr. Freed the following day. By the next week, I had completed his remarkable book and had an evaluation scheduled.

Jeffrey Freed was actually intrigued by Jamie. He was very optimistic and hopeful about Jamie's future, quite the opposite of what I was used to hearing. Beau accompanied me to the evaluation and was absolutely blown away by how much Mr. Freed knew about our son. He was able to explain his peculiar behaviors and struggles. He also explained how to use Jamie's strengths to overcome his weaknesses. Jeffrey pointed out that Jamie's whole world was governed by his right brain. In his book where he describes the left and right brain continuum, he explains that the right-brained individual is more apt to store information in pictures. He writes, "As nature gives the right-brained individual a strong visual memory, it also tends to diminish the ability to perform logical, linguistic tasks. While the right-brainer has a head start in the world of pictures, he's handicapped in the world of words. Unfortunately for him, our schools are primarily worlds of words."[17] In order to solve a problem, one must know what the problem is exactly. Beau and I were pretty sure Jeffrey nailed it.

Jeffrey began working with Jamie in the middle of seventh grade. He began strengthening Jamie's visual memory for the purpose of ultimate recall. He did this through memorization games, color coded spelling words as well as complex multi-step math problems. Jeffrey still works with Jamie to this day enhancing his incredible memory. Though they seem like simple exercises, this therapy has proven so very successful. Jamie has learned to turn his words into pictures and has progressed tremendously, especially with reading.

To this day, I sit with Jeffrey and Jamie absorbing all the valuable information I can. I can say Jeffrey has definitely educated me as well throughout the years. He has been instrumental in helping me find the right school for Jamie, continues to help me navigate the IEP process, and also gives me plenty of great advice with social issues. I love to say that God smiled upon us when he sent us Jeffrey.

One of his favorite sayings is: "A little bit of the right stuff goes a long way." He taught me to work with Jamie in very intense but short bursts. The important stuff being good sound writing, reading comprehension using visualization, and a few multi-step math problems. He taught me not to burden myself with extraneous details that were too complicated or would not serve Jamie in the future (reminding me of Charlotte Mason's infamous term "twaddle").

He also stressed the importance of being gentle and relaxed when working with Jamie to curtail all pressure. He maintains that the good nature of the teacher means everything and that this would be a crucial requirement if Jamie were to return to school. The first thing Jeffrey did when he started working with Jamie was to establish a good relationship that encompassed trust and endless tolerance. I believe this is why Jeffrey has been able to bring Jamie so far along. Jamie feels comfortable with him. He feels comfortable enough to succeed as well as comfortable enough to fail. There is always an environment of encouragement and acceptance present.

I found myself much more productive under Jeffrey's direction. I felt relieved and revived. As a result, I was able to teach Jamie things I never thought I could. I just had to search and pray for the right angle in which to approach the task, especially concerning math.

In math, it was high time he learned to calculate using long multiplication and long division. I did this by creating a step by step method that he could use every time without fail.

Once he had his multiplication facts down solid, I began to teach him two digits times one digit. I explained carrying and would draw an empty box over the number that was carried onto. This gave him direction and confidence. He practiced this for a couple of weeks successfully and eventually the box was faded out. I learned this model of teaching from one of my favorite math curriculums called *Mastering Mathematics* by Letz Farmer.[18] I did not subscribe fully to one curriculum but carefully picked out bits and pieces of good stuff from many curriculums.

The next intervention was given to me as an answer to prayer. I was quite overwhelmed by teaching Jamie to multiply two digits by two digits. I couldn't think of an easy way to simplify this. So, I prayed about it. The next morning, I grabbed a tablet and two highlighters, one yellow and the other orange. I highlighted the first number with the yellow highlighter as well as the two numbers he would "dance with." We multiplied these numbers and placed them in the first horizontal row colored yellow. (The carrying boxes were brought back where necessary.) The next number was highlighted with the orange highlighter along with his two "dance partners" and as they were multiplied, the answers were recorded in the lower horizontal column colored orange. After this, the yellow and orange columns were added.

It was visual, and there was a method to the madness every single time. It did not take him long to become proficient.

Long division was a bit of the same. I used the famous "Daddy Momma Sister Brother" acronym (DMSB for Divide, Multiply, Subtract and Bring down) and would work it with him step by step. We spent a long time making a trial and error chart of possible multiples to place in the quotient box, but after lots and lots of charts and extra work using this extraneous extra step, he was eventually able to do this one in his head without the hassle as he understood the process. It was actually my plan that he become tired of making the chart and start doing the math in his head.

Next, I had him master his multiples and factors, as I had taught Drew. From here, I had him practice finding the least common multiple between two numbers as well the greatest common factor between two numbers. After demonstrating proficiency at this, he was able to learn to add and subtract fractions as well as simplify them with ease.

Thanks to the internet, I found the greatest tool for teaching fractions: the Hershey bar. As each one is segmented, it was simple (and delicious) to teach about proper, improper fractions, and mixed numbers.

I tried to bring real life math into Jamie's world at every opportunity. I was forever giving him mental math problems to solve. I would give him scenarios where he would have to add up fast food items quickly and calculate the change back. I made sure that the scenarios were fun and interesting, involving him sharing pizza with friends or going on a date with a pretty girl to the movie. The beauty of these exercises was that we would practice in the car, on a bike ride, or even in the swimming pool. Without pencil and paper, he would have to create images, and that was even better suited for his learning style.

Yes, it took Jamie longer to learn these skills than most, but I knew my child could learn. In fact, I became convinced he could learn anything. He just needed time. And I gave him plenty of time. I insisted on complete mastery before moving on to new concepts. I was continually reminded of Ronald Davis' quote in his insightful book, *The Gift of Dyslexia*, "When someone masters something, it becomes a part of that person. It becomes part of the individual's thought and creative process. It adds the quality of its essence to all subsequent thought and creativity of the individual."[19]

Jamie had created an imaginary character called "Baldin." Though his teasing phase was essentially over, thank God, he thought this character was absolutely hilarious. He created this guy "Baldin" by shaving one of Lisbeth's Ken doll's head and dressing him up in a tuxedo. He gave "Baldin" a wife and a pet dinosaur as well as a best friend. It was kind of weird— okay really weird, but he started making comical videos with these characters about real life scenarios. It became his hobby. Even though I saw to it that Jamie had plenty of social interaction with friends during the week, I knew that he was meeting some sort of social need or using this as an opportunity to learn or rehearse. His videos were quite funny and appropriate so I did not stand in his way. In fact, "Baldin" helped me out quite a bit.

Jeffrey always says, "The offense needs to use what the defense gives them." So, I created a notebook labeled "Baldin's Adventures." Jamie would brainstorm ideas, and he would write a story about Baldin and his crew. Some of the titles included: "Baldin Goes to the Movies," "Baldin Goes to the Grocery Store," "Baldin Goes Skiing," and "Baldin Goes Camping." I would give him an outline and let him go to town using his imagination (which at the time was virtually nonexistent) and writing skills. We incorporated spelling, grammar, punctuation and format, as well as creativity, into these stories. It was a great success. Baldin was his character after all. He felt like he owned it and looked forward to writing these stories every day.

Seventh grade turned out to be very productive. Jamie was learning like crazy, Jeffrey Freed was on board, and I noticed a complete turnaround in behaviors, especially in social situations. He was enrolled in group competitive swim lessons as well as a homeschool P.E. class. He also continued golf lessons with nothing less than appropriate behaviors. I took him to play nine holes of golf practically every Saturday. Amazingly, he was able to maintain good golf etiquette and follow the rules. I swear I was witness to a miraculous transformation.

Jamie had matured to a level in seventh grade that far surpassed our wildest dreams. From the behavior, social, and academic problems that we had faced in the past, we were overjoyed at the progress he had made. The only obstacle now was the age old quintessential homeschool problem— he was literally dying to be back in school with friends in a classroom setting. He longed for it and begged to go back to school every day at the very end of our year. I felt compassion for him and came to understand that this was something he needed, so I prayed.

My prayers were quickly answered. Jamie's weekly homeschool PE class just happened to be held at a church where a school for homeschoolers met. It was a small charter school funded publicly for children who were homeschooled. It met three days a week teaching life science, applied science, humanities, math, and writing. I immediately sought more information on the program.

I discovered that the subject matter was very rich and significant. There was no twaddle there. Each and every class was taught "hands on" by experienced, patient, kind, and credentialed teachers. The days off were an opportunity for parents to step in and help with the assignments or supplement the learning.

This would be perfect for Jamie, but I had concerns. I did not know if he was ready to be back in a classroom setting without any support. I also knew he was far behind an eighth-grade level and feared the work would be too difficult.

I soon met with the director who was absolutely lovely, and she encouraged me to enroll him. Her view was that he would be in a very positive environment filled with the most compassionate teachers and the kindest children. She maintained that he could work at his own pace without any pressure or demands. Jeffrey accompanied me to meet all of the teachers so that he could make sure this was the right move for Jamie. He was quite impressed and gave me his blessing.

I did end up enrolling Jamie in Colorado Classical Academy for Homeschoolers. His eighth-grade year proved to be very successful. He was wonderfully behaved in the classroom. Though the academic work was beyond his ability, I did it with him, explaining as I went and holding him responsible for the work that he could complete. He took every test, completed all homework and every writing assignment. He even participated in the science fair. Yes, he had a ton of help from me, but he still participated and learned from the experience. Most of all, he learned to be a student—sitting quietly, following directions, and being respectful to his classmates and teachers. As far as I was concerned, that was enough. However, he did thrive academically as he was forced to read and operate independently in the classroom.

It was the best environment I could have possibly imagined. The life science class was completely hands on. I volunteered once a week in the classroom and witnessed many cool experiments. The kids learned anatomy through dissecting sharks. They had the opportunity to visualize and identify the structures of the heart through actual sheep hearts. They were taught to prepare slides and visualize cells using a microscope. They also learned genetics and intricate cellular functions through many fun and interesting activities. The class was real, it was functional, and it was dynamic. I remember thinking to myself, "What if all schools operated like this?"

The humanities class was quite special too. The teacher was a world civilization expert who used many different mediums to teach interesting facts. The kids were constantly making dioramas, posters and models of ancient dwellings. She even organized an archaeological dig. I helped out by clearing and weeding the plot of land for her. It was a great learning opportunity, and the kids ate it up.

The writing class was enriching as the teacher required a specific written paper each week. By the end of the year, Jamie had written over twenty papers. She also taught advanced grammar as well as Latin and Greek roots. It was at this time that I saw what a gift Jamie had for memorizing. He easily learned the definition of 120 roots by the end of the year.

The children there were very kind and accepting towards Jamie. He made some nice friends and thoroughly enjoyed his time at this little school. It was heartbreaking when the year was over. Colorado Academy for Homeschoolers served only fifth through eighth grade. I would have to start shopping for another school. I have to admit, I was quite anxious.

I knew exactly what he needed to succeed in high school. I could clearly define it. I just did not know if any such school existed. So again, I prayed. I asked the Lord to find Jamie's school. I was now pretty tired and needed to just have some blind faith.

I began to survey all the parents I was around for schools with excellent special needs/resource programs. I was given some encouragement about a particular high school in our district by a friend and decided to investigate.

I called the director of the Special Education Department at this particular high school and had a very long and interesting conversation with her. I was astonished and delighted to learn that she integrated these students in the regular classrooms for science and history with support while also teaching them English and math in special classes that utilized personalized small remedial groups. This was the perfect combination of school and remediation. She also used peer helpers (advanced students) in her English and math classes which I thought was pretty clever.

She was a lovely lady with a sweet nature who seemed like she had this down to a fine art. She had been there for years and had brought many struggling students along to where they no longer needed resource classes by their senior year. I was amazed and impressed by everything she said. I knew from this conversation that this was where Jamie needed to be.

The only problem seemed to be that this was the most desirable high school in the area, and many kids were on the waiting list, especially for ninth grade. She did inform me that he would have to make it through open enrollment.

I had Jamie's Nana and her Sunday school class praying for his acceptance as well as the rest of our family and friends. I did not have a plan B. I felt like God had directed my every step with Jamie all of this time, and there was no way He would let me down now.

I applied for the following school year in the winter and patiently waited but got no reply back. On many occasions that spring Jamie would ask me, "Mom, where am I going to high school?"

And I would answer, "I don't know yet buddy. I haven't gotten an answer back from Red Rocks High School."

He would look a little down every time we went through this drill.

One day he asked again and I just boldly blurted out, "Son, you are going to Red Rocks High School." It was a proclamation— I was naming it and claiming it.

Three days after I told him that, I received an email from this teacher inviting him to shadow the school. He had been accepted. It was May, and she wanted to give him the opportunity to check it out, as well as to see if he would function well in these classes. The whole staff was impressed with how polite and well behaved he was. His teacher was anxious to have him aboard this lovely group of very high functioning students she was mentoring.

Jamie would attend Red Rocks High School in the fall. I sent him donned in rock concert t-shirts, a trendy haircut and some cool shoes. Under the direction of some really great teachers, he would learn more than he had ever learned in his life, achieving the honor roll with his modified curriculum. He would make tons of precious friends and would even attend the Homecoming dance. It felt like a dream coming true, but I knew it was an answer to prayer.

## Lisbeth

Life is often times like a seesaw. As one side comes up, the other side must surely come down. As Jamie was finally learning and thriving in a homeschool/classroom setting, my daughter was pretty much drowning. She was also in eighth grade, attending our neighborhood junior high school, and facing some pretty difficult challenges.

Lisbeth had been involved in competitive cheerleading for about a year. It was quite a serious and stressful commitment. Though she enjoyed it at first, as time went on she found herself absolutely miserable. But the stress of cheer was just an exacerbation. School was also getting difficult, and there were many tedious and complicated assignments that left her completely overwhelmed. I would say, however, that her best friend in the world turning her back on her was the ultimate hurt. There were misunderstandings that Lisbeth knew nothing about, and a disheartening breech in confidentiality. All of this, coupled with a local school shooting as well as a foiled murder attempt at the high school next door, really shook my girl up. She began to have anxiety and panic attacks that were incapacitating.

My heart was so heavily grieved. I had to find some way to help her as she was in such a pitiful state. All I ever desired for her was to be happy and healthy. This is what I focused on barring all else. And if I had to completely rescue her from life, I figured there is no better time than these adolescent years to do so. I believe that this is the time that kids need the most help.

So I did what I have learned works best and implemented individualized targeted attention. I pulled Lisbeth out of school mid-year and homeschooled her. She needed to be home where she could be nurtured body, mind, and soul.

It was a desperate solution, but I had prayed about it and felt confident that this was the right thing to do. She always had to be the strong one. She was our good student with no learning deficits. She was the perfect daughter— socially acceptable, extraordinarily sweet natured, beautiful, and smart. I wonder sometimes if there was no room in our family for her to be any less than this. Her birth order was quite messed up as she seemed to take the role of the oldest in the family. I just felt that there was more pressure on her shoulders than she could ever explain. Her feelings were important. She was important. It was time that she received the attention that she needed.

I carried an extraordinary amount of guilt when it came to my daughter. I know that she was pushed aside many times due to all of Jamie's needs. I felt that she always knew she was loved, but did she feel significant? Did she feel valued and acknowledged? I needed to make sure that she knew how we really felt about her, so I prayed to the only One who could help. Yes, I received an answer.

My answer was at *Michaels* craft store. I proceeded to gather supplies and began making a personal and unique scrapbook highlighting the beautiful events of her life. It read like a story, and she was the star. Through this book upon every page was the truth that we adored her, and she was indeed a very important and valued member of the family.

Lisbeth spent the remainder of the school year with me. She was primarily expected to read, write, and do math. We worked on physical science together, and independently, she worked on a large U.S. history timeline where she listed historical events chronologically and illustrated them with her great artistic talent. She read five great novels, writing outstanding papers on each. And with a hefty amount of practice and a good curriculum, she completed Algebra I.

The time we spent together was priceless, and I feel it was as important to her as food, water, and shelter. It took a long while for her to recover from the crippling anxiety, but we began to see her thrive and gain confidence. As we discovered, it was definitely a spiritual attack, and we handled it as such. With good Christian counseling, involvement in a life-giving youth group at a local church, some wonderful friends, and an amazing trip to the Grand Canyon, where she witnessed God's glory first hand, she began to come back to life.

She re-entered public school at a smaller and more traditional high-school in the ninth grade and hasn't looked back since. Her confidence is being restored daily as she is learning the real truth about herself. I would say about her today, with all praise belonging to God, she is most certainly happy and healthy.

I enjoyed every minute of homeschooling my children. These were some of the best years of my life. It was interesting, fun, and exciting to explore the world around us. I loved learning right along with them and ended up with quite an education of my own.

The homeschool experience blessed all of our lives. It brought Drew confidence, Lisbeth a new sense of self-esteem, and Jamie an opportunity to have an independent and productive life. I am sure that educating our kids is a primary way to honor and please the Lord. I will continue to pray for good schools and curriculums void of political rhetoric and opinions. I will also pray for the good teachers to have a safe place where they are autonomous in teaching what is really important.

## Chapter Seven
# Hidden Sins

*"Lord, now indeed I find thy power and thine alone, Can change the leper's spots and melt the heart of stone, Cause Jesus paid it all to Him I owe, Sin had left this crimson stain, He washed it white as snow"*

—*"Jesus Paid It All," Elvina M. Hall (1865)*

One of my dear friends, who has gone through some pretty tough times, was confiding in me that she really didn't feel comfortable in church anymore and hadn't had a church home in over a decade. She felt that so much in her life had happened that she just couldn't bring herself to sit there in the pew. I perceived this to mean she didn't want to sit there like a hypocrite. I began to tell her that I understood that oh so well.

The reality now is that I sit there as the most fallen sinner in the room. I know that not one of us deserves to be in the presence of the Lord. When I sit there humbly as a repentant sinner desiring forgiveness and change, only then I can abide.

Embracing my fallen nature as an opportunity to be crafted by the Maker has led me to confront some significant matters of the heart. I have realized that "hidden sins" such as pride and unforgiveness separate us from God. They are indeed invisible, and the enemy habitually lies to us making us feel as though these sins are minimal. One of the most profound truths I have discovered is that sin is sin, and no one is immune.

Aren't we all guilty? I will tell you my heart has been so injured by pain from the insensitive words and actions of others that I have lived with intense feelings of anger. My heart actually has the capacity to harbor contempt. How is that less than stealing, lying, adultery, or envy? I don't think it is.

The enemy definitely uses pride to make us feel self-righteous and above reproach. Should we ever have the right to dismiss our sins because they are invisible and judge the ones who sit with theirs in plain sight? The reason we are all invited and welcomed is because Jesus invited us. He invited all of us. He offers Grace to all of us. Only Jesus knows the heart of man. Only He can forgive. Only He can vanquish, and only He knows. We should never allow Satan to burden us with this sin of false pride.

Though I am aware that I am bathed in unconditional love and acceptance, I have struggled with such sins of the heart. I am most definitely still a work in progress as the Potter is not even close to being done with me. The truth is, He has molded me through my sin just as effectively as He has molded me through my pain.

It's not pleasant to revisit, but there came a time when I looked in the mirror and did not like the person staring back. I had adopted a negative spirit, and I was a mess. I was struggling with much repressed anger stemming from an unwillingness to forgive. This was a terrifying time. I did not know what to do about it. I couldn't just snap my fingers and make the madness dissipate. I could not pray it away, nor could I perform enough good works to change this blackness in my heart. Sin had strangled me and moved me so far from God I was absolutely miserable. It rendered me helpless and lost. And just because my sins weren't overt and on display, they were still sins of the heart— as destructive as any.

Through much prayer, I came to the understanding that this anger and resentment came from being deeply hurt by people I trusted, being overburdened, and chronically exhausted. I had literally worked myself into a state of madness. I was stuck in a service frenzy as there were way too many people pulling on me. I had a bad habit of continuously putting way too much on my plate and became furious when everyone kept adding to the pile. This had become a way of life for me.

Yes, I have always loved the Lord, but at this time in my life, I was finding it really hard to love others. This drove a very deep wedge in our relationship.

By the time I said "Uncle!" I was willing to do anything. I was desperate for God's love to permeate my soul and fill what cannot be filled in any other manner. I didn't care what I had to suck up, admit, or who I had to unwillingly cater to; I wanted my relationship with *Abba* back. Confronting my sins and ridding myself of them was the way there. I, never wanting to be the Pharisee that I so despise, was just that — withholding compassion and being unwilling to forgive.

# Attacks

Shortly after I started homeschooling Drew, I had two significant dreams that were basically the same. These dreams were unusual in that they were both very vivid, and I recalled them days after with intricate detail.

I was being bitten by dozens of snakes continuously. The strangest part was that no one could see them because they were under my clothes. I was miserable, but I did not fear death because I was aware that the snakes were not poisonous. Knowing this did not keep me from feeling terrified. As I looked around, I noticed that I was the only one being bitten. My husband was just fine and could not understand my agony. In fact, my family appeared to be quite content and happy. They did, however, stop from time to time to ask me what was wrong.

The second dream was just like the first one except I was made aware that chopping the heads off of the snakes was the only way to make them stop biting. (No doubt, spiritual dreams can be quite strange.)

I was quite disturbed because, for the first time I felt like my family was stable and headed in the right direction. The kids were happy and healthy. We had a plan for Jamie. Beau and I were getting along quite well, and I was feeling hopeful for the future. I knew without a doubt that these were significant dreams. But what did they mean?

I pondered the dreams for a few weeks. I did not tell anyone about them because they were just too weird and creepy. After praying for a couple of weeks, I decided to share them with my friend Lorie. She is the only other person I knew that has had spiritually significant dreams. We had been friends for a long time, and I knew that God had gifted her with discernment. I knew she would take me seriously.

She immediately pointed out that the snakes were God's way of revealing to me an intense spiritual attack. It was a spiritual attack that would not lead to death (the snakes were not poisonous) because I belonged to Jesus. However, the attacks were sure to render me completely miserable and immobile for a time.

I realized later, through prayer, that identifying and dismissing a particular sin in my life would allow me to chop the heads off of the snakes. This would be my way through the attacks.

I was certainly warned…and misery soon followed.

## Anger and Resentment

Towards the end of the homeschool years, the snakes began to bite. I began to enter a dark phase of my life I call the "great madness." It was a time where I felt mad at the world. I was emotionally spent and had absolutely no tolerance for anyone's nonsense. Mostly, I was sick and tired of everything in my life being so hard. Everyone's expectations of me were also draining. It was though no one saw me struggling. No one could see how much of my life I had sacrificed. Though I still very much adored my children and loved caring for them, I became callous, cold, and sarcastic to much of the rest of the world. I complained a lot and became very negative. I was truly a mess inside.

I had been overextended for way too long. The truth is I really did do everything. I did everything for everyone all the time. I was exhausted and eventually became exasperated by a plethora of bad attitudes when I finally did attempt to say no.

Yes, I morphed into this despondent, irritable being. But there was a history. There was much unresolved conflict that I endured and unwillingly accepted in order to stay committed to my task at hand which was creating a stable, loving, enriching home.

It is true that I had been treated poorly from time to time by a few of the people that I am closest to. I had been hurt deeply and did not deal with my feelings, but instead buried them deep down inside where they would fester. I always knew they would resurface, and when they did it would not be a pretty sight.

I finally became so overwhelmed that I really didn't want to be around anyone but my children and husband. I had absolutely nothing left to give and crawled deep into my isolated rabbit hole. I was fighting to recover my son and to maintain a healthy household on a day by day basis. I could no longer bear the strain that self-centered people placed upon me.

The only role I knew was that of "the giver." I never had any time or any money, but that never kept the demands at bay. I remember hearing the chaos swirling around my head…. "I need…. I want…. Would you mind…" Who knows, maybe the anger was a defense mechanism that kept me from having a nervous breakdown.

I was a mother of three children including one with significant needs. I had made four moves by this time. My husband worked long hours and was out of town quite a bit. I also had to educate my children at home who were falling behind in the school system that was failing them. I had virtually no support at all. I had almost no time to spend with friends or participate in anything fun or relaxing. Life had been way too hard for way too long. I was spent.

I had no time to take care of my own needs. I think the worst part was not having anyone to lean on. I grew very bitter. It was a period of my life that I am very ashamed of.

## A Little Compassion Please?

No one could possibly know how hard it was to raise a child like Jamie, day in and day out. The elementary years proved to be very tough. He wasn't a baby anymore, and people weren't always tolerant.

No one could possibly know what it felt like when he dug his hands into the middle of a child's birthday cake at a party, or worse, when he took a leak right there out in the middle of the park. He would throw potted plants into my brother's swimming pool, tease the neighbors who had been through a divorce or were bereaved, and say the most inappropriate things he could think of to anyone that would pay attention. He would routinely pull the stuffing out of all of my couch cushions, pull all of my neatly folded sheets out of the closet, or destroy things just to see me gasp. I had to limit playdates with the other two children because he would break their friend's toys or completely humiliate them on every single occasion.

I was a basket case for many years. I followed him around constantly trying to keep him out of trouble but also trying to interact with him and teach him things. I repeated things over and over to him as he had significant trouble with auditory processing. I would explain until he verbalized his understanding. It was years later that I saw my husband counting on his fingers after I spoke to him, and I asked, "What are you doing?" He snickered when he proceeded to tell me that I repeated everything that I told him three times. My mother also told me she was worried that I had early Alzheimer's disease because of this same thing. I wasn't sick, and I had no neurological deficits. I was simply conditioned to intervene for my son ALL THE TIME. No one could understand.

Life with Jamie was hard. I endured much scorn and much criticism mostly because I knew there was a function to his behavior. I never once failed to discipline him in some way for naughty behavior, but I felt sorry for him because I understood him. One of his major challenges was that he had little impulse control when he went to the birthday parties because he was overstimulated and in a new environment. His little nervous system would shut down if he didn't know what to expect. That little voice inside his head that said, "Jamie you can't just whip it out and pee in the middle of a crowd," was on a temporary vacation. So was the one that told him he needed to wait politely for his slice of cake. He was taught social etiquette on many occasions, and I was becoming an expert on social stories, but some people didn't consider this. Some automatically assumed my child was a savage and that we cared less about correcting him. It was painful, but I hurt mostly for him. In time, he stopped getting invited to birthday parties altogether. As for me, my dignity was last on the list of problems and very short lived.

Keeping the other two children in a healthy, thriving environment where they had opportunities to learn and grow was another very difficult task. I had to take Jamie with me wherever I went. There was no one willing or capable of keeping him. It was a nightmare taking him to the grocery store, not to mention Drew's baseball practice, Lisbeth's ballet recitals, or piano lessons. Lisbeth and Drew also found it challenging to maintain friendships.

I also had Jamie in tons of therapy that was time consuming and costly. Lisbeth and Drew had to constantly ride along and eventually became resentful. My middle child had a festering problem of her own. She constantly felt like we loved Jamie and cared for him more. No matter how we argued that fact, Lisbeth was a little child and could never understand. She felt slighted, I felt guilty, I overcompensated, and another issue was born.

Even the people closest to me could never understand the life I lived for so long. I felt like they didn't notice. It seemed I could not run fast enough or jump high enough—there were too many expectations. For many years, I did whatever was asked of me. I was always the one that would step up to the plate. But that began to change as I entered into a season of bitterness. Galatians 6:9 instructs us not to "become weary in doing good…" I can admit I did a lot of good for a lot of people, but I was now definitely weary and completely spent. Everyone in my life exhausted me, and I wanted very much to be left alone.

What I needed most was to raise my own family, run my complicated household and be free from everyone else's burdens. After a while and out of self-preservation I had to become unavailable. It took a while for me to get there, but a long history of suppressed anger that stemmed from a big, ugly, root of bitterness helped me out quite a bit.

I found out the hard way that the root of bitterness is not one that is easily overcome. I prayed endlessly for years for God to change my heart. It was Psalm 51 that I prayed so often. I even placed a calligraphy sticker on my bathroom wall that read, "Create in me a new heart o' Lord."[1] (I was counting heavily on the stick-on phrase to do the trick.) But my heart never changed. I continued to be internally angry.

There were a couple of years where I just unloaded on people. I yelled at my sweetest friend and my niece. I even socked it to the lady at the grocery store because I couldn't find the biscuits. I remember going off on her saying, "I couldn't find anyone in this place to help me. I've been walking around for an hour looking for the biscuits, and do you know where I found them? Next to the beer. What's going on? Do you alphabetize the food? Last week I came in, and you didn't even have cabbage. You don't ever carry buttermilk. I'm sorry, this is just not working out. It's not you; it's me. It's over. We are through." My daughter was with me, and after a period of utter shock and embarrassment, loves to tell the story about me breaking up with the grocery store. I wish she would forget it. I never wanted to become that person.

What I eventually had to realize is that my state of mind, health, and happiness was mine to own. It was certainly no one else's problem. I began to try to investigate hidden sin in my life in order to please the Lord and to prepare for His blessing. Nothing happened. I was still angry, resentful, and bitter towards the world. I truly hated me. I wanted to run away, but I changed my mind when I realized I would have to take myself with me.

The answer came as the Lord inconspicuously whispered to me. I then knew He expected me to do the work. The anger came from somewhere. This was not my nature. He created me with a big heart— loving, kind, and selfless.

I truly cared about people and would go to any length to help anyone in need. Being ill-tempered and rude was not my nature. What happened to me? What was causing me such emotional stress? I had to earnestly examine my conscience to realize that I needed three things: to forgive generously, to rid my spirit of pride, and to start setting some healthy boundaries. My negative attitudes were beginning to affect my children and my dear husband. Our home, that I struggled daily for years to keep peaceful and happy, became anything but. I had to take responsibility for the state of my heart.

Forgiveness became essential. I could not move on without it. Some very hurtful things had been said and done to me over the years, mostly when I was so vulnerable and weak. I had no problem forgiving, it was that I was reminded over and over again of these hurts as the insults continued. I was simply tired of dealing with everyone's bad behavior. I couldn't seem to help wanting to rival it. I was also tired of constantly forgiving and just gave it up. With good counseling from the Holy Spirit, I came to realize I just had to forgive once. I had to realize that the behaviors of others will probably never change. It was my behavior that I had complete control of. I finally turned it over to God and prayed a blanket prayer of forgiveness that included the past, present, and future. It was an easier pill to swallow when the Lord showed me that forgiveness is not about me or them. It was about loving Jesus. And this I could do.

Brennan Manning beautifully explains in *Abba's Child*, "Experientially, the inner healing of the heart is seldom a sudden catharsis or an instant liberation for bitterness, anger, resentment and hatred. More often it is a gentle growing into oneness with the Crucified who has achieved our peace through His blood on the cross."[2] And that's exactly how it happened.

I found that loving God with all my heart and soul, essentially my sole purpose in life, could not exclude loving my brother. That as God extends compassion, so should I. As God readily offers forgiveness, so am I expected to do so. The problem was that it felt impossible to me.

And Manning answers in *Abba's Child*, "The demands of forgiveness are so daunting that they seem humanly impossible. The demands of forgiveness are simply beyond the capacity of ungraced human will. Only reckless confidence in a Source greater than ourselves can empower us to forgive the wounds inflicted by others. In boundary moments such as these there is only one place to go-Calvary."[3]

## Forgiveness Sweet Forgiveness

God has an extraordinary way of transforming our hearts and minds and teaching us especially through compassion.

When we first moved to Denver, we lived next door to Nicholas Mendoza, a very wise, capable man of invaluable resources. He was a professional tracker with many skills. We were intrigued by his life experiences and noted the sheer goodness that he exemplified. Over the few years that we were neighbors, we grew close to him and his sweet family. After Beau and I had moved to Houston, Nick landed the job of his dreams in Rwanda, managing a Christian school founded by God through a lovely lady who happened to be in my bible study class.

This school was ministering to the children of the very poor and vulnerable survivors of the devastating genocide of 1994. It was a brilliant design to educate the future generations as well as provide employment to the families. To this day, I am so very partial to this effort because it provides opportunity which, in my mind, is so much more valuable than charity.

I had little knowledge of Rwanda's history or tragedy in 1994. Nick was working full time in Rwanda doing nothing less than a yeoman's job for the school and the community there. Beau and I had not seen him in a few years and were blessed when he paid us a visit during our first Christmas back in Denver. He briefly explained the history of the genocide and recommended a book,

*Left to Tell,* by Immaculee Ilibagiza.[4] I was mesmerized with his tales of this land and ordered the book immediately.

I was spellbound with every word, and I read the book in one night. I could not put it down. It spoke to me and touched my heart deeply. It is a true account written by a genocide survivor, narrating the horrifying innocent slaughter of over a million people. I found the book to be a beautifully written, inspiring tale of faith and forgiveness.

There's nothing like a good genocide tale to set one's priorities straight. I was convicted and knew that God had spared this precious lady, Immaculee, to tell her story, one that would impact the world. With the exception of one brother, she lost her entire family during this heinous event. She hid in a tiny bathroom with eight other women for three months to escape certain death.

Her tale of God's love, provision, and her supernatural ability to forgive is unforgettable. Surely, if this woman is capable of forgiveness so incomprehensible, I should be ashamed to deny it to anyone, at any time, and under any circumstance.

It took some time for my heart to thaw out, but I did learn from Immaculee. I learned that forgiveness is life-giving, and to withhold it brings much suffering and misery. Her saving grace was knowing the sacrifice God made when He sent his very own Son, Jesus, to die on the cross for all of us. The agony and pain God felt losing His very own precious and blameless son to die an unjust death, she could identify with.

As difficult as forgiveness may be to dole out, there is never an excuse to withhold it. I learned through Immaculee, that with a willing heart, the Holy Spirit can even grant it supernaturally when we are unable.

A dream came true one evening, at a fundraiser for the Rwandan school, when I had the great privilege of meeting Immaculee. She spoke for over an hour about faith and forgiveness. It was so powerful, I could feel the presence of the Holy Spirit as tears streamed down my face. Her words moved me because I knew they were inspired by the Creator. I couldn't wait to have her sign my book. I was hoping she would hug me and somehow transfer this massive faith to me through osmosis or something.

She was quite tall and very beautiful. Her voice was rich and eloquent. Her movements were graceful, and there was an aura that surrounded her. When you were near her, you could feel that you were in the presence of someone very special.

I had tears in my eyes when she signed my book. I was eagerly anticipating the hug that would dry my tears and infuse me with the gift of faith and forgiveness I so longed for. But as she tenderly looked me in the eyes and hugged me, she whispered, "Pray for me." I was baffled.

Wait! I'm the victim here. I need help. My heart is broken. It's all about me. Right?

Wrong! It was about genuine compassion for others and about extending the empathy that I had longed for so long to someone else. I had to give in order to receive. What a blessing she gave to me after all. This realization would eventually change my heart and strengthen my faith.

As she writes in her second novel, *Led By Faith*, "Faith is a living thing that must be nurtured every day through prayer, kindness, and acts of love. It will lead us through our darkest days and restore love and light to even the most troubled soul in the direst circumstances."[5]

At this point in my life, I needed, truly needed for the first time. I felt wounded inside like a victim of post-traumatic stress syndrome. I had been so deeply hurt, I did not know if I could recover. She taught me that God is there to heal and restore, but His power is only unleashed through forgiveness.

Immaculee teaches in *Led By Faith,* "Hatred, anger, mistrust and fear enter our lives every day in a thousand different ways. We're all wounded by these evils, but we can all be healed through the power of love and forgiveness— a power readily available to all of us when we have faith."[6]

To this day, I continue to pray for Immaculee in her never-ending journey of forgiveness. She also inspired me to expand my intercessory prayer life. I have a Christmas card holder where I place all of my beautiful Christmas cards during the season. I cherish looking at my beautiful family and friends all season long, and I'm known to leave it up sometimes until Easter. It breaks my heart to take them down as they bring me so much joy. I decided after praying one day, to take them down and put them in a pile. This pile I would shuffle through every morning while praying for each family.

This act of compassion, putting others needs before mine, has blessed my soul and softened my heart.

## Self-Pride and Boundaries

Practicing forgiveness was definitely changing my heart, but I felt God was not going to wave His magic wand and dismiss my anger and resentment. There was much work to be done, and so the Potter got busy.

He wanted to change me by changing my attitudes and habits. These feelings did not mysteriously appear nor would they immediately vanish. My Father knows that in order to be happy and content, I need to rely on Him and acknowledge His strength and power.

For most of my life, I covered up my feelings of inadequacy, shame, and guilt through a false sense of self pride that convinced me I was capable of "saving the world." My self-pride had to go. It was time to start saying no; this entailed letting go of ego.

In Matthew 18:3 Jesus says, "Truly I tell you, unless you change and become like little children, you will never enter the kingdom of heaven." To me, this means coming to Him innocent, fresh, and available to be molded—easy for the unformed child, not so easy for the tainted adult. In order to be molded, we must be humble and void of ego.

In the New Testament's book of James 1:17 we learn that "Every good and perfect gift is from above, coming down from the Father." What a relief! I had to embrace the fact that I could not take credit for anything remarkable that I did or said. If it was good, it was of God. Truly, this was liberating.

I eventually learned to set healthy boundaries and ignore the criticism. I had to learn to refuse to be offended. But most important, I had to finally lay down this self-pride. I had previously believed there were no limits to my abilities. Many times, I expected too much of myself and not nearly enough of God. I had a lot of work to do to get these sins out of my life. The Lord would help me change my heart and revive my family; I was certain.

I had to admit that I could not do it all. I was not always available. I was not always responsible for everyone's happiness, and I did not have to be perfect. Through the cross, Jesus freed our souls from death in 33 A.D. It was now time to free myself from expectation. I was not nearly as capable as I thought I was.

There were a few very difficult relationships that I had to address. People often times, do not like it when you start saying no. I have to admit, I did not handle it well at first. I became a little rude and exasperated until I was able to fall into a rhythm where I didn't feel the pressures of guilt. Stiff-arming everyone for a period of time actually flushed out the problematic relationships. I was able to start relaxing with those who respected my "no's," while continuing to reinforce tight boundaries with those who became spiteful as a result.

This is how sinister the enemy is and how determined he is on stealing the joy of the believer. During the height of my "great madness," my beautiful Jamie really started to heal and blossom. He was finally recovering from the depths of autism. I had found a wonderful school with competent teachers who really cared for him and knew exactly what to do to help him. Though he was still academically behind and needed much support, they believed in him and were dedicated to helping him reach his potential. It was in ninth grade that we really started seeing him turn the corner. His social skills improved dramatically, and he became the most polite, loving, and thoughtful young man anyone could ever meet.

Clearly, the enemy was desperately trying to steal our whole family's joy. This was a time when our family should have been recovering and healing from all of the difficulties we had endured. Lisbeth was doing great in school, had great friends, and was gaining some much-needed self-esteem. Drew also surprised us with how well he was handling middle school, as hard as it can be. He was making good grades, good choices, had great friends, and was really starting to care about school.

I looked outside of my misery and finally saw what was happening. I had to call it for what it was, and then the real battle began—the one I was not a part of.

# Idolatry

Another sin standing in my way of peace was idolatry. I had always put my family a priority over God. They became my idol as I lived to serve and worship them. I loved the Lord my God, but sincerely I tell you I did not love Him with "all my heart and all my mind." There was not room. I put God in my back pocket as my family became priority number one. A little late in my journey I found out there was such an easier way to live.

What I have learned is that when God is first in my life, is seems as though everything else falls neatly into place. Specifically, if I start my day in worship and in awe of Him, I have peace, I feel strong and capable. I feel hopeful about the future because I know He is in control, not me. This very special time in the morning sets the tone and the success of my entire day. I also feel strongly about giving God our "first fruits." At first awakening, putting Him at the top of the "to do" list is honoring this.

Worshiping Him, praying, and claiming His promises also nurtured my broken spirit. I had neglected self- care for so many years. Everyone's needs came before mine. When I put God first, He filled the part of me that could never be filled with a hair appointment, a manicure, or a lunch date.

I came to God relentlessly needy. I was so ashamed of my condition. I had always been so valiantly self-sufficient. How strong I thought I had always been but how broken and spiritually poor I actually was. When I finally started prioritizing my life and reflecting on what I needed emotionally, I felt like I needed compassion most of all. I had so much for others. I needed the people in my life to realize how difficult things were for me and how hard I was trying and give me a break, but they rarely did.

I eventually came to realize that God had compassion for me, and it was enough. He knows the depths of my heart and my desire to please Him. I began to seek the Lord and beg for His presence. In him, I found a remedy indeed. In accordance to His Great Compassion, He lightened my load and added no burden. Through continuous prayer and contrition, I came to understand that He was enough. He loved me unconditionally through this hard time and bathed me in forgiveness and mercy. My prayers of Psalm 51 He did answer— on His time.

God was, indeed, working on my behalf at this time. During this time that I was praying for compassion, He opened my husband's eyes. Beau rose up and became my champion. He nurtured and cared for me at this time demonstrating more love than he ever had. He listened to me, helped me, and treated me like gold. I had all I needed, just one person who understood and had my back.

Out of all of my struggles, this "madness" was the absolute worst. For when I was grieving over Amelia, I clung to my Lord and refused to let go. He was in every fiber of my being. When I had almost lost my mind with fear and anxiety over Jamie, though my faith wavered, I still felt the presence of the Lord because my heart was innocent and pure. As I wept and pleaded through the "sadness," of course He was there— for "The Lord is close to the broken-hearted and saves those who are crushed in spirit" (Psalm 34:18). But during this "great madness," Satan was at his finest. He attacked me so heavily, there were times I could not feel God's presence.

I'm not saying that God would ever leave me, only that the evil spirit had to be conquered. I came to realize that life is a constant spiritual battle for the believer. I faced a daily battle of the mind where I would start to think negative thoughts and immediately call on Jesus to rebuke them. I shortened it to "JESUS!" that I would shout in my mind. That was my code word for deliverance. He fought for me. All I had to do was ask.

Yes, again and again my Lord delivers me. I definitely do not deserve it; but thank God, we don't ever get what we really deserve.

Identifying the hidden sins in my life and working hard to rid myself of them has not only stopped the majority of the spiritual attacks but has brought me a greater level of peace and contentment.

## Conquering Weariness

It's easy to spout off platitudes and words of encouragement and faith, but weariness of the mental, emotional, and physical kind must be given the proper attention. For it is real and must be conquered.

Weariness of life often strikes the parent of a special needs child at some point. Few can understand the day by day chaos or the minute by minute struggle you deal with for years in some cases. It causes a state of alertness and a constant flood of adrenaline that can really affect our delicate biochemistry. In any case, the end result is exhaustion—mentally and physically. As profound as it is there is no way to describe it.

As I most definitely suffered from this, I finally found a valuable remedy to weariness. I began to purposefully enter into God's rest. It is a place where the only priority is loving, worshipping, and listening to the One True God. Though the concept is very simple, it's not as easy as it sounds. You must create a space, make a time, and enter with a willing heart.

As ironic as it sounds, I conquered weariness through running. I feel most at peace when I'm outside on a long run. My house has so many distractions. It feels nice to be away. When I am outside, surrounded by God's beautiful creation, it is quiet, calm, and I feel peaceful. I need this environment to be alone with Him in a capacity where nothing else matters. It's as though I run away from all of my fears, inadequacies, and shame, asking God to forgive me and strengthen me. As I run back home, I see the beautiful Rocky Mountains, the blue sky, and brilliant sun. I always run home at a stronger pace, singing praise songs in my head, feeling as though my joy and strength has been renewed. It has proven to be miraculous therapy.

Most difficult is creating a time. It is really hard with all of the demands placed upon me, but I had to learn to prioritize. It helps me to ask myself the question, "What is more important than my relationship with God?" It's healing therapy that improves my mood and restores my positivity. My family sees this and is very glad to acquiesce. There is always forty-five minutes in our day to step away if we prioritize it.

Entering God's rest is not possible without a willing heart. I remind myself that I am the clay in His hands. I am welcome to bring my anxieties, hurts, and failures to the party, because I know that in a spirit of surrender, He is faithful to save me from myself. When I ask God to remove the burdens, He alone has the ability to transform my heart into a willing and peaceful state.

No doubt, I am a constant work in progress. I don't always concede my life willingly and I don't always recognize when I need Him, but I'm getting better every day. Nevertheless, this is the truth, and when I allow Him to restore me, He never fails. What a life-giving gift!

# Disappointment

I wish I could write about all of my trials and tribulations in a positive light so that I could model my beautiful, calm, patient, and gentle spirit for all the world. But that would be the worst kind of fabrication. I did not always handle my battles in this way. Many times, I succumbed to defeat by giving up, weeping pitifully, feeling hopeless, frightened, and angry.

All of these feelings result when we lose faith. Losing faith in times of strife can open wide doors for the enemy. The great deceiver benefits from our anguish and hopelessness. What I am learning is that, though we are believers in Christ, our outcomes are not always optimal, and things do not always go the way we plan. Sometimes our most valiant efforts fail—miserably. Even with the "dream team" of faith, righteousness, love, and obedience, things still go wrong.

People can still be unkind and sometimes cruel. Expectations can be destroyed, and sometimes utter chaos and disaster strike. The truth of the matter is that this happens. Things go wrong all the time.

To quote Dr. Greg House, my favorite atheist and the fictional star character in my all-time favorite T.V. show *House M.D.*, "Good things usually happen but bad things sometimes happen."[7] They do, and randomly at times. There are many things over which we have very little control. However, we cannot have our faith fluctuating up and down like frequency waves without any stability. We can't just swing from full faith when our outcomes are good, to non-existent faith when outcomes are poor. Our faith has to remain constant or we will truly live as a prisoner of circumstances.

One of the greatest gifts we receive through faith is peace and contentment. Paul, the famous evangelist in the New Testament, while being jailed and beaten reveals in Philippians 4:11-12, "...for I have learned to be content whatever the circumstances. I know what it is to be in need, and I know what it is to have plenty..." To me, this is the greatest gift of all. Contentment, I have found, is the antithesis of disappointment.

I am hopeful that I will, day by day, learn to be content, relying on Him for my peace. I must also be mindful of how deeply He has loved me through the toughest of times.

## Chapter Eight
# What's Going On?

*"Turn your eyes upon Jesus, Look full in His wonderful face, And the things of earth will grow strangely dim, In the light of His glory and grace."*

— *"Turn Your Eyes Upon Jesus,"* Helen
Howarth Lemmel (1922)

"Just because you are crazy, this doesn't mean you are wrong."

I always laugh when my husband tells me this. Being a right-brained individual, I often see things in a different light. I have a keen discernment about situations. I happen to believe it is attributed to my best quality which is being pure of heart. In any given predicament, my motives are always sincere. I have no agenda other than to love and care for my family and honor my God. I can usually see right through hidden manipulations and self-serving motives. Perhaps some could call me a conspiracy theorist. I guess they would be right. I believe life is actually one big conspiracy. Everyone wants what they want, and they continue to conspire to get it. The key here is: find the agenda—find the truth.

I don't think that I am alone when I say that something is definitely going on. There is indeed an autism epidemic, and I believe it is time to start asking some hard questions.

# Vaccines

Most of my passions in life are focused around autism because, as a mom, I have seen something tragic happen to my child right before my very eyes. I have observed, read, looked, and learned with a passionate intensity for a long time. I have come to my own conclusion about autism. (And because it is of my opinion, I'm hoping to still be protected under the first amendment.) Without using the scientific method or any formal research, my opinions are of the "duck" kind. If it walks like a duck, quacks like a duck, looks like a duck, and smells like a duck ...guess what? It's probably a duck. Duck opinions are not researched based. They don't require extensive trials, money, publications or fraudulent controls to be appreciated. They are my form of "deducktive" reasoning and I consider them as valid as any. The power of observation, sound reasoning, and discernment, coupled with lack of selfish agenda are some pretty strong research tools.

Our government loves to say that diagnostic criteria and diagnoses have changed over the last twenty years —that there is no autism explosion. This is the biggest fabrication of all. They tout this being the reason for the increased number and startling statistics of this disorder. But I know that parents of autistic children would differ. No matter how you played around with the words or labels, these children would have been easily identified even a hundred years ago. Another truth is that 80% of people on the autism spectrum today are under the age of twenty-one.[1] We have to know the truth in order to change this trend.

All of this to say that I consider the cause of autism a "perfect storm." There is much evidence of a genetic predisposition that concerns the detoxification pathway that I don't deny. The MTHFR gene mutation, which Jamie and I are both heterozygous for, is proof enough for me. But this is only the "spark"(tiny chemical reaction) which can easily grow into the full-fledged flame of autism with the right catalysts.

One of the major catalysts, I believe, is the childhood vaccination schedule. I strongly believe there are too many, too close together, too young. They are also laced with known neurotoxins such as aluminum, formaldehyde, benzethonium chloride, and thimerosal (amongst other names that I can't pronounce).[2] These ingredients alone can cause neurological abnormalities. Another risk with vaccinations comes with the assault on the fragile immune system of the infant. Live viruses provoke an immune response in our systems that defends against harmful invaders. If the human immune system gets overloaded with T- cells, inflammation is always the result and can have negative effects on the developing neurological system of the neonate, in particular.[3]

There is a wide spread belief in the scientific community that the "blood-brain barrier" of an embryo, fetus, and a newborn is immature or leaky. The blood-brain barrier in the human brain is a tight junction of endothelial cells that line the brain's interior blood vessels. It creates a semi-permeable membrane designed to protect our brains against toxins, bacteria, or viruses. The belief is that the function of the "leaky" barrier in early life is to allow for more nutrients from the placenta and breast milk to be readily absorbed and delivered during this crucial time of brain development. I must say— God is brilliant.

It makes me want to cry thinking that what God designed ultimately for good, in my opinion has become a vehicle for the rise in neurological dysfunction we are seeing today in jaw-dropping numbers. I do not believe that these neurotoxins injected into our infants through vaccines are insignificant. Stephanie Cave, M.D., writes, "The timing of infant and toddler vaccines...corresponds to critical periods of neuronal development. The blood-brain barrier is not fully developed in the infant or toddler." As parents we must consider this—we must be our children's most dedicated advocate.

My biggest beef with vaccinations is the agenda behind them. Vaccinations used to be so necessary for health, and now they have become an agenda for wealth. The government conspiracy with the major pharmaceutical companies is so far and wide, I doubt anyone even knows the real story anymore. Like a good John Grisham novel, the common good is deceptively used as a prop for evil corporate/government greed. Do I believe that the push for vaccines is part of a sinister plan for big money? A resounding *yes*! And it's all about the duck.

Let's take a common sense look at vaccinations. We are all bullied heavily and are actually told that our children might die horrible deaths without them. I would like to know the answer to two questions before I proceed. How many children, in America, have died from a disease that could have been prevented by a vaccination they failed to get? And, how many children have had all of the vaccinations they are required to have and are now on the autism spectrum? I truly don't know the answer to the first question, but I intend to find out.

I know that "herd immunity" is a popular complaint with physicians and pharmaceutical companies. Their grievance is that unvaccinated children have protection from diseases due to the fact that others that surround them are vaccinated, but the whole concept is misrepresented. Originally, "herd immunity" was used to describe a community where most of the people contracted the wild form of a disease and developed a lifelong immunity.[5] This is very different than "vaccine immunity" in which individuals have to receive periodic boosters of the vaccines, testing their titers to see if they are still protected from time to time. There is no lifelong immunity with vaccines. The potency and effectiveness of vaccines are always in question. In a community with "vaccine immunity" there are still periodic outbreaks of diseases such as measles and pertussis from time to time.[6] Truly, one would have to have a lifelong steady influx of vaccines to stay immune. Herd immunity has been misrepresented.

The second question I have an answer for: The CDC released data on March 27th 2014 showing that 1 in 68 children in America has been diagnosed with an autism spectrum disorder, specifically, 1 in 42 boys and 1 in 189 girls.[7] Despite public and congressional outcry, "There has never been a controlled study comparing long-term health outcomes of vaccinated and unvaccinated populations" as explained in the informative book *Vaccine Epidemic*. One would wonder, why not? The data doesn't seem like it would be very difficult to obtain, and it would sure put the nail on the coffin of the vaccine controversy once and for all.

One of my many problems with the whole vaccination push is that I fail to see the logic in many of them. Hepatitis B is a blood born pathogen. That means the risk factors include sexual contact, intravenous drug use or blood transfusions.[8] Now how many newborn infants have the risk factors for this disease? But the clincher is knowing that its effectiveness is estimated to last approximately ten years when given at birth. As the population approaches an age where the risk factors start become legitimate, the vaccine loses efficacy. Furthermore, the CDC touts its sustained efficacy of twenty years IF given at an age greater than six months old.[9] There is absolutely no beneficial reason to give it at birth.

Another problem, in my opinion, is diphtheria. From the years 1980-2011 the incidence of diphtheria averaged between one and two cases per year, and since the year 2000, only five cases have been reported.[10] It seems to me that our children would not need five boosters as the disease is practically eradicated. Though it is still identified as a problem in some areas globally, why not push for the vaccination for those traveling abroad. Or why not insist that every immigrant who enters the country receive it? Why is such a burden placed upon an infant whose immune system is so immature and vulnerable?

Another newsflash: tetanus is NOT contagious.[11] Yes, it can cause lockjaw and that is very frightening, but what is the CDC's main objective? It is not a communicable disease and the length of the effectiveness is always under question. Also, the shot can be given immediately in response to possible contamination in this country where hospitals are easily accessible. Why does the CDC care so much? Why do they insist on giving it to a newborn? And why do they lump an appropriate, justifiable vaccination called pertussis in with tetanus and diphtheria?[12]

Pertussis (aka whooping cough), is a menace to babies and the elderly. Though it is treatable, it can cause death in some cases. Half of babies with this disease are hospitalized and it is highly contagious.[13] It is a reasonable recommendation, but why is it only offered as a three in one? It is not available as a single dose vial. It is offered only as Dtap (diphtheria, tetanus and pertussis). In order to receive it, your baby's immune system has to contend with three bacterial toxoids— basically, three poisons that act as the disease but don't cause the disease, resulting in great immune responses and subsequently overwhelming inflammation.[14]

As for the mumps, measles and rubella vaccination, history shows fewer side effects and greater safety from the following two scenarios: administering each as a single dose vial which eliminates harmful preservatives and increasing the age of the vaccine recipient to three years or older.[15]

A dedicated gastroenterologist named Andy Wakefield researched this extensively and published his findings in the British medical journal called *The Lancet* in 1998.[16] Many parents he encountered were shouting from the rooftops that their baby's severe gastrointestinal disease and subsequent diagnosis of autism coincided with the timing of the MMR vaccination. So, he listened to these parents, did his own research and published his findings. He most importantly stressed that the MMR be given in separate, single dose vials for safety reasons. (It is important to note that immediately after the publication of Dr. Wakefield's article, that all single dose vials were suddenly removed and unavailable in Britain.) He eventually lost his medical license and tarnished his reputation for life.[17] He never advocated against vaccinations. He simply researched a safer way to vaccinate. It's quite simple; the government should make it their business to know that these scenarios will greatly diminish a child's chance for developing autistic spectrum symptoms. They simply will not give it due attention. Why?

One step in the right direction was the removal of thimerosal in the vaccines beginning in 2003.[18] The thimerosal hype was indeed, in my opinion, warranted. It is a neurotoxin that was previously used as a preservative in some vaccines, including the flu shot and the Hepatitis B trio.[19] Mass immigration in our country, along with a failed health care system, places undue burden on the government to supply large numbers of vaccinations for children. Preservatives are necessary in multi-dose vials, and multi-dose vials are cost effective. However, even though the drug companies agreed to remove this preservative from future vials, the existing vials at the time were allowed to be exhausted.

There is no possible way, in my mind, that this form of ethyl-mercury when injected into our babies was not an implication in the autism explosion. I believe the proof is in the pudding. Yes, we still see rising rates of autism, but the spectrum has become much broader and more varied. The face of autism seems to have changed. The most severe cases of nonverbal, self-harming, very low functioning cases were diagnosed in the 1990's when thimerosal was present in large amounts. In my personal opinion, we see more Asperger's type, higher functioning diagnosis' today. Although I am convinced it is huge, thimerosal is only one piece to the puzzle.

Research is so very subjective that it's truly hard to get a clear answer to anything due to the intense bias of the source. If you would look up "thimerosal" today on the internet, you would find out through government sites such as the CDC or the NIH that receiving vaccines with this preservative is safer than eating a tuna fish sandwich.[20] Parents of children with autism would vehemently disagree. (I must also strongly caution anyone against arguing with the parent of an autistic child.)

The government claims it's the organic "methylmercury" that is so very toxic and that the "ethyl" form of mercury is not that poisonous. The ethyl form of mercury is a derivative from the methyl.[21] Furthermore, if a multidose vial of flu vaccine containing thimerosal is accidentally dropped and broken on the floor, the entire facility is to be evacuated, and a hazmat crew in full gear like a scene from a science fiction movie is immediately called out to the scene.[22]

The government started regulating thimerosal in the vaccines around 2003 due to intensive research and lobbying by some dedicated parents. Unfortunately, my son was born in 2001 and received his first of many doses of thimerosal in his second day of life. At that time, thimerosal was present in the Hepatitis vaccine (in three separate doses), and also present in the flu vaccine.

Another problem is that some of these vaccines are suspensions. The vaccines containing thimerosal separate upon standing, and if not properly mixed in the hands of the administering nurse, a child could be bolused with a large dose of ethyl mercury.[23] There are many complications that are too carelessly dismissed.

There is also the consideration whether thimerosal can be passed in utero from mother to baby. In 1993, I was injected with all three doses of the thimerosal containing Hepatitis B vaccination as required when I started my nursing career. No one can argue that this lethal poison is not easily excreted.[24] I don't have all the answers, but I am thankful this particular neurotoxin has been removed from most childhood vaccines.

I am not anti-vaccine. I do, however, believe in a carefully thought out approach in regard to them. I would like see extra money spent on single dose individual vials of all. This would eliminate the need for the harmful and poisonous preservatives. If you spread them out one at a time, you can note side-effects to that specific vaccine, identify the problem and correct it. Also, I think we can delay most vaccines and space them out thoughtfully. Finally, I think it never necessary to give any shot laced with powerful adjuvants (substances that provoke a greater immune response to an antigen) to a newborn infant.

There are certainly ways to vaccinate our children safely and effectively. If we don't pay attention and the trends continue as they are now, we could see a majority of kids on the spectrum in the coming years.

Here is what I know to be true. Genetic testing shows that I do have a heterozygous mutation in the MTHFR gene as Jamie does. I am certainly quirky, right brained all the way, and get overstimulated easily. Could this be the spark? The main difference I can see is that the vaccination schedule of the 1970's was a totally different story.[25] I was vaccinated with mumps, measles, rubella (in separate doses), tetanus, diphtheria, and oral polio, once as a baby and once before I entered school at four. The vaccinations I received did not contain thimerosal either. Jamie received twenty-five doses of vaccines (containing dangerous adjuvants and known neurotoxins) by the time he was thirteen months old—and that was just the beginning.

In my own experience, I definitely saw critical changes in Jamie's behavior and health after each whopper vaccination. The biggest changes I noted were after the MMR I also feel like the flu shot was the final straw for him. It seems, in hindsight, that he would recover a little bit after each round of vaccines. When assaulted again, he would regress. I believe this explains the rollercoaster of good periods and bad periods that baffled us all. After the flu shot, however, there seemed to be no more "good periods." Perhaps this was an overwhelming toxic load from which he could not recover.

It is true there has been plenty of research negating the link between autism and vaccinations. Still, I am unimpressed. My overwhelming skepticism seems to revolve around one issue—the entities providing the research all seem to have an iron in the fire.

The reason that I question whether immunizations are safe is due to the fact that all the research we have is provided by pharmaceutical companies and government agencies like NIH and CDC. This poses a problem because on February 22, 2011, the US Supreme Court made a decision exempting drug companies from all liability for harm caused by vaccines. It's called Russell Bruesewitz v. Wyeth.[26]In my opinion, completely relinquishing the drug companies from all responsibility for any harm caused by vaccines just seems sinister. If Pharma is not held accountable or liable for injury, then what motivates them to perform valid, time-consuming studies assuring they are safe for our children?

As a mother and a nurse, I feel I have the right to form a hypothesis about what happened to my child based on knowledge I have obtained through a plethora of education on the subject as well as the first-hand experience of being there. What if it happened like this: what if my infant son, genetically predisposed to faulty detoxification, received the thimerosal laced Hepatitis B vaccination on his second day of life, burdening his immune system and causing an auto immune response which opened the door for wild and crazy histamine release. What if this oversensitive immune response led to Jamie's allergy to the casein in his formula that furthered the inflammation and became the culprit of many ear infections— also leading to many other food intolerances as he started to ingest solid foods. What if the massive antibiotics given for the endless ear infections enabled an overgrowth of bad bacteria aiding the formation of his "leaky gut" which exacerbated his immune deficiency by preventing his little body from absorbing crucial nutrients? And what if just in time, at one-year old, the MMR vaccine is given while his immune system is completely haywire and overwhelmed? What if his immune system is not equipped to contend with this virus resulting in measles in the gut and subsequent brain swelling? What if this happened to coincide with his hindered development, loss of language, and indifference to me and those around him. What if his immune system, so brilliantly designed by God, starts to recover slowly but then gets waylaid by the massive dose of thimerosal he received via the flu vaccine at three years old? What if the toxic load at this point was just too much for his body to handle? What if this flu vaccine was indeed the straw that broke the camel's back? What If this was how it happened? What if this was the reason I lost my little boy to an empty reality for so many years?

What about my other two children? Yes, Lisbeth received most of the same vaccinations as Jamie, but on a much more spread out time table. Also, the NIH, itself, actually conducted research that suggests that estrogen is protective against the adverse neurological effects of mercury on the brain.[27] Perhaps, it is wise to hypothesize that this may be the reason boys are five times more likely to suffer from autism than girls. What I can say is that she became terribly ill immediately following her flu shot at two years of age. She developed mononucleosis and was sick on and off for about a year after.

Drew was born in 2003. It is possible that thimerosal was removed from his initial vaccinations. I also ceased vaccinating him after his twelve-month MMR, and he never received the flu shot. It is also plausible that neither Lisbeth nor Drew have the predisposing genetic make-up.

So, what is my motive? Do I have one? Yes, I most certainly do. My motive is not to find blame or fault so that I can more easily navigate through the stages of grief into the acceptance phase and move on with my life. It is not to find an excuse to exercise my righteous anger. It is definitely not for attention or notoriety. My motive is simple and clear cut. My desire is to see my child and others affected restored to their fullest God given potential. I want the trend to stop. Learning what I have about vaccinations has given me the opportunity to make really good informed choices. Because of the valuable research from other dedicated parents, doctors, and scientists, I know the truth and have avoided giving my child the recommended vaccinations on the recommended schedule. I wholeheartedly believe that this has enabled Jamie to greatly recover from this most cruel and unusual disability.

My prayer for the future is for our country's government to take the blinders off and to see a real problem. I pray that more wasted tax dollars be spent on valuable life-giving measures such as creating single dose vials of good quality vaccines —that those accountable err on the side of caution in creating the schedule, considering autism as the same level of risk as the diseases themselves, and that profits from this particular industry be eliminated. Under these circumstances, I would vaccinate all of my children according to the appropriate recommendations.

## Mercury in Dental Fillings

There are three types of mercury; elemental, inorganic, and the organic form as in the vaccines. "Silver" or "mercury" dental fillings are properly called amalgams. These fillings are made from a combination of metals such as silver, copper, and tin, as well as the elemental (or metallic) form of mercury. (The mercury comprises around 50% of the compound.) They proved to be very durable and long-lasting— thus, widely used by dentists in the past.[28]

I never gave the idea of elemental mercury in my mouth much of a thought. As I began to research autism heavily when Jamie was around four, I started reading a bit about this. I was focused on healing his digestive issues at the time so I did not pay much attention.

In the summer of 2005 I was working at Vacation Bible School (V.B.S.) at our church. Early in the week I developed a really bad toothache. One afternoon when Beau came home from work I visited a local dentist. As he took a look inside my mouth he gasped and remarked, "You have a leaking mercury filling in your mouth." I had only two fillings in my mouth and otherwise had a history of great teeth. He explained that he needed to replace the leaking filling immediately with a composite filling and proceed with the root canal on the neighboring tooth that was causing me pain. He was quite baffled that I needed a root canal. He remarked how strong and healthy my teeth were.

He did the necessary dental work and all was well until that Friday at V.B.S. when I developed a very painful urinary tract infection. I called a friend who lived out of town who was a physician and talked him into prescribing an antibiotic for me. He was hesitant because he is very prudent and judicial when it comes to medicine. Nevertheless, I was scheduled to work all weekend at the hospital and begged him for the medicine that had worked so well before. He was gracious and called the medicine in.

The infection seemed to be getting worse over the weekend. I worked back to back twelve-hour shifts, and though taking the medicine faithfully and drinking tons of water, I was getting worse. On Sunday morning, I began taking ibuprofen for the pain. By Sunday late afternoon, the ibuprofen had worn off and I immediately started going down the tubes. I felt like I was dying. I had a fever of 104.5 and could barely walk. I immediately checked myself into the E.R.

180

After collecting a urinalysis and some bloodwork, the doctor claimed it was the worst urinary infection he had ever seen and that it had spread to my kidneys. I begged to go home on oral meds but he told me that if I left the hospital I would die. He insisted on admitting me and starting I.V. antibiotics immediately.

For three days, I received I.V. antibiotics running fever so high that the nurses' aid had to change my ringing wet sheets about three times a day. I remember I could not even lift my head up off of the pillow. My diagnosis was acute pyelonephritis, which is a very serious kidney infection.

Thanks to the great medical care, I recovered just fine. However, I continued to question how I could have gotten so ill from a simple urinary tract infection. My doctor friend was right. I should have initially had a urine culture to determine the appropriate antibiotic, but I still wondered how It could have escalated to that extreme so quickly.

I did recover but remained sickly for the next couple of years. That winter I developed pneumonia for the first time in my life. It seemed I was continuously plagued with strep throat, colds, and viruses. It was several years before I actually felt vibrant and strong again.

For the next couple of years, as I researched the forms and potency of mercury, I began to formulate a belief of what had happened. I came to understand that the kidneys have an extremely hard time filtering this substance from the blood.[29]

When the dentist removed the amalgam that had been poisoning me in small doses for who knows how long, he was not skilled in mercury free dentistry and did not use the appropriate protocol that would have prevented massive doses of mercury from flooding into my digestive tract and entering my bloodstream. It is possible that the kidney infection came first. In my opinion, I believe this massive dump of mercury could not be filtered properly by my kidneys and caused the dysfunction which gave way to this overwhelming infection.

I cannot prove this. I cannot give scientific data to confirm what I know to be true. And of course, the serious infection that followed the mercury ingestion could have certainly been a coincidence. I can only offer my honest opinion and my most sincere belief. To me, it walked like a duck and quacked like a duck.

## Trends in Modern Medicine

I see pervasive changes in the attitudes that govern modern medicine today. New pharmaceuticals and technological advancements have taken center stage as the medical field has become very lucrative. My biggest concern is with medicine. I am concerned with the trend of moving towards pharmaceuticals to cure every ache, pain, discomfort, or foul mood. The "whack-a-mole" syndrome has gotten out of hand. I was made painfully aware of this during my twelve years working as an R.N. Every medicine has a side effect. Like the arcade game, it seems as when one symptom is whacked with the hammer, another pops up. Pretty soon there's a lot of whacking and one train wreck of a patient. This is symptomology medicine, and I believe it to be potentially dangerous, especially with the over prescribing of antidepressants, mood-altering drugs, sleeping pills, and narcotics. Of course, medicine has truly been a godsend and has saved many lives. I am very thankful for the antibiotics that saved my life. I am also thankful for the innovative, new cystic fibrosis medicine that is saving my youngest niece's life. I'm only advocating a risk-reward analysis concerning the use of some of these pharmaceuticals. I believe that diet, exercise, and sleep habits have been laid by the wayside and dismissed as viable interventions for some illnesses.

Vaccinations have been treated in the same way. There are no big strides being made to boost the immune systems of the community but instead to waylay them with as many vaccines as they can come up with. There seem to be no big strides being made to treat the root causes of diseases either. In many instances the goal of medicine seems to be about abating symptoms. Perhaps the Hippocratic Oath which promotes the philosophy "Do no harm" has been antiquated. (By the way, many medical schools are now actually tailoring their own Hippocratic Oaths to fit their own new-age belief system.[30]) I don't have all the answers, but I can share the experiences that have shaped my thoughts.

As my daughter, Lisbeth, approached ninth grade and needed a health physical to participate in cheer tryouts, we made an appointment and visited our pediatric group. It had been at least a year or two since we had been there, and a new female doctor was attending to her. After the very in-depth questionnaire, the doctor gravely looked at me and insisted that I start my daughter in counseling merely from the fact that she expressed she was unhappy with her weight. My daughter had not weighed herself in six months and was surprised at the changes she was noticing from a huge growth spurt. Ignoring the arguments from me that: my daughter did not exhibit any signs of a body image problem at home, she was a healthy eater, she was at a perfect height and weight, and most importantly she was fourteen years old, this doctor gave me a very long lecture. She was quite adamant that my daughter needed counseling. I felt like I was in the twilight zone where logic and reasoning had vanished. So, I was cool about it, pacified her, and kept on reading my magazine until we got to the second issue.

The doctor asked my fourteen-year-old daughter if she was sleeping well. My daughter said no, that she found it hard to fall asleep at night.

Being that it was the middle of the summer, I tried to reason with the doctor that Lisbeth had gotten into a habit of staying up very late at night and sleeping in very late in the mornings. I laughed it off understanding the mindset of a teenager.

I was carefully taught in pediatric nursing to observe and give great value to the developmental stage of the patient when taking a history. It was obvious that this doctor did not understand the mindset of a teenager at all, and she began a very serious lecture about sleep that lasted around ten minutes. As she wrapped it up, she offered sleeping pills as an option if things didn't get better. My eyes got as big as saucers. Now I'm thinking, "Is this a joke?" Nope, she was as serious as a heart-attack.

Next it was vaccines. I really tried to play it cool. I did not want to go there, but she prodded and insisted that I tell her why I chose not to keep Lisbeth's vaccinations up to date. I began by telling her that my daughter had been fully vaccinated in the past but that the ones that were recommended at this age, I felt, were unnecessary. I kept trying to move the conversation forward and change the subject. I have always kept my feelings about this topic very personal and private out of respect for our physicians, and I never wanted to be labeled as an "anti-vaxxer." She simply would not let it go and insisted that we go over every recommended vaccine and talk about it. (Lisbeth giggled later in the car that she knew it was going to be "on" when she saw me take my glasses off and put my magazine down with a sigh.)

We discussed the HPV vaccine and the Tdap as well as the bacterial meningitis vaccination. She reluctantly accepted my reasons for all except the bacterial meningitis. She tried to explain the disease process but did so with great inaccuracy. I was stunned but did not correct her. She also patronized me by explaining how deadly this disease was. At this point I had no choice but to chime in informing her that I was well aware of the severity of the disease. I had taken care of two patients in my nursing career with bacterial meningitis. I knew that this was a ravaging disease with a high mortality rate. We used to implement serious respiratory isolation as we knew it to be highly contagious and deadly. I risked my own safety taking care of these patients for months at a time. Yep, I knew all about it. She was a fairly young doctor, and I wondered if she had ever seen a case. It is very rare, which brings me to the point I was making to her.

I feel that you can't protect children, much less anyone, from every danger. There are so many devastating diseases and senseless tragedies in our world. There are risks everywhere we turn. There is a risk sitting in a movie theatre, going to a concert, and now even sitting in a school desk. I ended on a gentle note when I said that I would re-evaluate the vaccine when my daughter entered college, very carefully assessing the outbreak statistics.

My breaking point came when I gave her my thoughts on the Hepatitis B vaccination series making my case about how unreasonable it really is for a newborn baby. The woman who had been more or less bullying me for the last thirty minutes actually put her hand over her mouth and whispered, "I know, I didn't give it to my own children."

I was utterly disgusted but left without incident. I could feel my passions ignite and the fire in my belly rising up, but I left quietly. I didn't want to start out so right and end up so wrong.

All of this to say, I feel that we, parents, must be an advocate for our children and question the logic and reasoning behind everything, especially medications and vaccinations.

# Food

Food, no doubt, has implications in the autism epidemic. Mass food production has led way to the birth of G.M.O.s (Genetically Modified Organisms) known to be treated with dangerous herbicides.[31] Also present are poisonous preservatives in our food supply. I call this our "chemical diet." Mass food production started around the time of World War II. Seventy-five years, in the grand scheme of things, is not really that long ago.

As I think about genetics being the spark and vaccines being a catalyst in the "perfect storm" of autism, I think about our "chemical diet" being the fuel to the fire. Food certainly does not cause autism, but consuming unhealthy foods full of bad stuff can definitely make the symptoms much worse. This is what I have learned from my own personal experience.

I also have found that going "all in" on a highly restrictive diet was no long- term answer either. I have found gluten free, dairy free, sugar free, and paleo-type diets to be super beneficial as a short term (two to three months) cleanse. But for the long-haul in our busy world, you have to make decisions that you can live with that aren't impossible or unreasonable. I eventually settled into a lifestyle of good dietary choices for my family. I try to buy organic as much as possible, and I buy food with limited ingredients (that I can easily pronounce). I also try to make as much as I can from scratch. This is not always possible, but I give myself a lot of grace and an "A" for effort. I do have some "musts" as well as some "absolutely nots" on my staple food list. I also try to avoid everything packaged in a box.

Our world seems backwards to me. It doesn't make sense that our generation is so gravely concerned with the environment as though this is the most pressing issue of our time. Most people even believe that the manner in which we are living is somehow contributing to climate change. I'm not so convinced that we have the power to impact the climate one way or another, but I do believe that we can impact the human condition.

Though I am well aware that we are expected to be good stewards of the world that we live in, I feel that our bodies are temples of the Lord and should always have priority over the earth. How is it possible that our society is so passionate about our responsibility to the environment, but could care very little about the poisons that we are injecting into our babies and the poisons that are placed in our food for financial gain?

# It is What it is, So Go Ahead and Build a Bathroom

"If you tell a lie big enough and keep repeating it, the people will eventually come to believe it." (Joseph Goebbels—propaganda master)[32]

There is no autism epidemic. There is no autism epidemic. There is no autism epidemic.

The first thing you will hear from the "experts" is that autism has always been around. My question is: If there is no crisis, then where are the statistics on autistic adults? Knowing very well there are adults diagnosed with autism— I just can't seem to find any data on them. If we could see the age statistics in a visual graph, our thought processes, as a society, might actually change.

I am also inclined to believe that the rhetoric that doctors are just getting better at diagnosing it and this is the reason for the rising numbers is pure malarkey. They sure get exponentially better at it each year, don't they? In fact, research scientist Stephanie Seneff, of Massachusetts Institute of Technology (MIT), predicted in 2014 "At today's rate, by 2025 one in two children will be autistic."[33]

The spectrum is unusually vast, encompassing many diverse, multifaceted diagnostic criteria that seem to change with every passing day. (The criteria moved from having 12 characteristics on the list to 6 for a clinical diagnosis here recently.) Is the mystery, perhaps, that what we are seeing is not truly classic autism but rather neurological damage? Is this the reason we can't put autism in a box and must classify it as a spectrum disorder as big and wide as the Grand Canyon? I don't think that this condition we are liberally labeling autism has always been around.

Trends are definitely my biggest ally in this argument. The trends are what persuade me most. They have me convinced, and to me, are more reliable than the grandest research and studies conducted by the CDC, the NIH and the pharmaceutical companies all put together. After all, how valid can we treat these studies performed by the very entities that have skin in the game?

The CDC informs us that in the 1970's and 1980's autism affected 1 in 2500 children.[34] I believe that to be a very generous number. I never knew an individual with autism growing up, and the first time I ever heard the disorder named was watching the movie "Rain Man" in 1988. In 2007, it was reported that 1 in 150 children were affected.[35] In March of 2012, the rate was 1 in 88.[36] Then in March of 2014 the CDC released a report showing 1 in 68 boys were diagnosed.[37] And Now in 2017, not an official statistic from the CDC but a new government National Health Interview Survey is revealing 1 out of 45 boys are affected.[38] (It is important to note that the increase in numbers correspond with increases in the numbers of vaccines added to the schedule.)

In Anne Dachel's 2014 book *The Big Autism Cover-up*, the case is made that the media is lying to the American public about the startling increase in the prevalence of autism. She writes, "The public has been conditioned to accept that, regardless of the jaw-dropping rate, there's never a real increase, and by now the numbers simply don't matter. The rate could be announced at 1 in 25 and news outlets would still have officials saying it was due to finally getting the numbers right."[39]

There are many ways to explain away the autism crisis; not just underdiagnosing but also my all-time favorite: "It's always been here." With enough creativity and manipulation, you could rationalize it any which way you want.

In his best-selling book *Neurotribes*,[40] the thoughtful and kind-hearted Steve Silberman proceeds to inform us of the notion that autism has always been prevalent— it is simply a natural genetic variation that has evolved out of a technological necessity. He uses history and the tech bubble, specifically in Silicon Valley, to prove his point. He makes the point that we, as a society, must accept "neurodiversity" and celebrate it. Though there are many parts of his book that I truly enjoyed, I must adamantly disagree with this theory.

To believe this well-thought-out epiphany, one must first believe there is no problem—there is no autism epidemic. The fact that 1 in 68 children born today are socially handicapped, prefer to isolate themselves and unusually perseverate on a few narrow interests is a natural progression of the human race.

Well, that gets big Pharma off the hook. It also gives the "chemical food" industry a free and clear pass as well. So, who is left to blame? Intolerant neurotypicals— that's who. It is society's duty to create sensory friendly restaurants, malls, movie theatres, and more. Perhaps, we should even legislate special sensory friendly bathrooms designated with a puzzle piece on the door.

If nothing is happening to our children, then we should feel ridiculous for researching and investigating. If nothing is happening to our children and autism is just a natural progression of life, then we should give up trying to change this trend, fully embrace it, and just make the appropriate accommodations. Even many T.V. programs are embracing autism in an attempt to weave it into the fabric of our lives, conditioning us to accept it as the norm. If we are tolerant enough, have enough resources, and get enough of those puzzle piece bumper stickers, we could actually make an autism-friendly world.

I say hogwash. This disorder called "autism," as my son experienced, is not a societal problem. I believe it is neurological damage that resulted from a vulnerable immune system unable to contend with a massive overload of toxins and stress. And I would vehemently disagree that that this neurological damage should be celebrated— not after what my family has experienced. This cruel and unusual condition has tortured my child. He missed out on the first five years of his life. He was essentially absent. He looked so sad and far removed from the world that his mother cried herself to sleep every night for at least a decade. His father's back should be broken by now from the financial strain and responsibilities he has willingly endured all of these years— sacrificing every dime he had to countless therapies and tutoring. His sister and brother have also endured many hardships that kids should never have to bear. Jamie's meltdowns were so intense that our home felt like a war zone for many years.

If nothing "happened" to Jamie's brain, then how was he able to escape the chokehold on his life—the incapacitating symptoms that this condition produced? If there was nothing wrong to begin with then how could he recover?

I am confident to call Jamie "recovered" by my standards. He will always be on the spectrum, but not strangled by the symptoms that threatened to strip away his life. Yes, something happened, and we fought and taught and prayed and payed with everything we had to "recover" our child. I will never forget that something happened.

Autism is indeed an epidemic. There needs to be a "wake up and smell the coffee" moment for our society. We must listen most intently to the parents of these kids. For they are the greatest historians, the greatest researchers, and the most valid, agenda proof source we have.

As a parent of a once severely affected child, I can tell you I have had my boxing gloves on for a long time, and I don't have any plans to take them off. I have single handedly taught my child almost everything. My husband and I were always, as most parents are, completely invested in our child— emotionally, financially, and spiritually. We had to believe out of faith that God would usher us out of the darkest moments if we kept pressing on. It was not easy. There really wasn't much help for us. We finally got tired of emptying the bank account, living on love, and started helping him ourselves. The idea here is that we didn't wait for society to change—to offset the balance in our child. We did not waste any time playing the blame game either. We did the hard work ourselves. We had no choice. We simply did not have the means for an autism therapy filled lifestyle as we had two other children to support. Our son is one of the finest men on the planet, however, I would never wish this hardship on another family as long as I live. I enthusiastically celebrate the man my son is, but I do not celebrate what we experienced to be "autism." It can be a heartbreaking condition, and the children and the families who are affected can really suffer.

After all is said and done, I do now embrace Jamie's eccentricities with open arms. He is refreshingly different. He is candid, truthful to a fault, and feels no internal pressure to conform for coolness sake. He is the most thoughtful person I have ever known, and to debunk the common misconception, he has an abundance of genuine empathy. He is a delightful young man with a beautiful personality. I would even venture to say he is a new and improved version of humanity, and our whole family is blessed because of it. These differences are part of who he is. They are unique to Jamie and make him so very special. These are not the differences that ostracized him from society, kept him locked away inside himself, and caused him and others pain and misery. Because we believed that something happened to our child's brain, we acted and intervened. We came to realize that recovery was possible. Beau and I love our son exactly as he is, nevertheless, we will always fight for his ability to live a life full of all the joy and happiness he deserves.

There is a big difference between appreciating the adorable and refreshing quirks of those on the autism spectrum and accepting the destructive and pathological effects of this disorder that wreak havoc in their lives. I don't believe we really want to strive to embrace the future of neurodiversity. I strongly believe we are obligated to love, accept, and help the generation already affected but work like crazy trying to isolate the catalysts responsible. Let's admit that we have a problem. We do have a responsibility to the next generation, and it's a big one.

# Education Reform

I believe we have an extraordinary opportunity and obligation to serve the precious children who are now affected. These are special kids with unique talents who have long been underestimated. So how can we help them reach their fullest potential?

I cannot say enough about education. Our children on the spectrum need an education specifically tailored to their right-brained learning style. Education is their lifeline and cannot be undervalued. Bringing new ideas, concepts, and a variety of joys to their world, in my mind, is the key. May we teach these kids so much good stuff that they are bursting with reinforcers— the things you love to do and live for.

Hobbies and interests are the great reinforcers. These are the things that captivate you and compel you to finish your work so you can relax and enjoy yourself. We all have them. Mine is playing the piano. Beau's is sitting down with the guitar picking out Led Zeppelin riffs. Some love to work in their garden, fish, cycle, bowl, hike, or draw. There are many ways in which to enjoy life to the fullest. Our spectrum kids need these hobbies. When they don't come naturally, we must facilitate them. They are the key to motivating our kids on the spectrum. I believe education brings forth life and is the most important way to reach in and pull these kids out of no man's land.

Education reform is needed desperately for all of our children but especially our spectrum kids. As much as I loved the benefits of homeschooling and saw the amazing impact it had on my child, I knew Jamie eventually needed school. He needed a good school that could meet his needs and enrich his life to a degree that I never could alone in our home.

Creative, right-brained oriented schools are definitely in demand. We need these schools to navigate outside of the box, foregoing stifling national education standards. In his book, *Creative Schools,* Ken Robinson outlines the need for a change in the way we are educating our children. He argues: "The fact is that our children and communities need a different sort of education, based on different principals from those that are driving the standards movement." He also explains, "People do not come in standard sizes or shapes, nor do their abilities and personalities."[41] Paying due attention to our right-brained oriented children, he writes brilliantly about "personalizing" education and highlights the steps necessary to make this happen:

- Recognizing that intelligence is diverse and multifaceted
- Enabling students to pursue their particular interests and strengths
- Adapting the schedule to the different rates at which students learn
- Assessing students in ways that support their personal progress and achievement[42]

I believe we can wisely invest in such schools specifically tailored for our spectrum kids. I feel it is imperative to put all of our eggs in the education basket. Let us invest in educating the kids instead of educating society—creating a sensory friendly world that addresses only the symptoms, leaving the root causes and much needed interventions essentially ignored.

To begin this process, the first thing we need is invested, inspiring, and dedicated teachers. They must be given input and autonomy. Robinson explains, "Too often the standards movement casts teachers in the role of service workers, whose job is to "deliver" the standards, as if they were a branch of Fed Ex."[43] They must be empowered to create the right conditions to cultivate learning. Perhaps, we could create competition so the indispensable teachers would see increased wages. We need teachers with an overabundance of patience, self-control, and unlimited compassion. These are the teachers that will make a difference. My child has had teachers with these qualities, and they were the most productive and most enjoyable years he had in school.

Standards must be tailored to the individual in the case of our spectrum kids. Qualified teachers and parents together should have the full autonomy to formulate a plan with the best interest of the student at heart. ABA therapy should be available to the tax-payer, as well as Sensory Integration (of highest importance to create an environment in which these kids can learn), and speech. A life skills class is also of great value. There should be an importance placed upon imparting knowledge creatively in a constant flow all day long, not simply abating unwarranted symptoms. As well, the curriculum must be meaningful and relevant.

In my experience homeschooling Jamie, everything I taught him had to be relevant. I noticed that he learned by making connections and stringing them together. Dr. Jane Healy is quoted in Freed's *Right-Brained Children in a Left-Brained World* explaining, "one of the biggest gaps in children's experience these days is in seeing connections between all the bits of information they have accumulated; teachers are frustrated because their students have difficulty linking ideas together meaningfully. A fragmented curriculum does nothing to remedy the situation."[44] We need integrated curriculums to keep our kids engaged.

Student-teacher ratios should be at an all-time low giving liberal access to direct instruction. Low student-teacher ratios are always costly, and this is the ultimate deterrent. Jeffrey Freed in *Right*

*Brained Children in a Left-brained World* makes the case, "While I recognize that lowering existing ratios will be costly, I believe taxpayers would be willing to pay for it if we finally see some positive results coming out of education."[45] Money spent up front on children in their developmental years (when they need the most intervention) will save tax-payers dollars down the road in regards to social services and mental health needs.

To combat the age-old attention deficit problem found with many students, I believe that rich and interesting subject matter is a must. Freed explains the significance of this as he writes, "Students can be captivated for large blocks of time if the subject matter is relevant and varied."[46] Art, cartoons, dioramas, and clay modeling can all be effectively used to teach our visual learners. Sometimes it is necessary to step into their world in order to bring them out to ours.

Also, I feel that the IEP (Individual Education Plan) that our public schools use must be re-invented. This is an overrated document that, in my opinion, was created to be a blessing, but in Jamie's case turned out to be a curse. It sounds brilliant—an individualized plan with detailed goals and outcomes to specifically meet the child's needs. Though the idea is heroic, I have actually seen the IEP as a hinderance to my child's learning. The goals on Jamie's IEP have been so obscure and long-term that it seems that day to day learning gets lost. I have been under the assumption that the most important function of the IEP is that it be measurable and that the progress be well documented. This is great; however, I sometimes see that the general education goals are forfeited, and this serves as a justifiable excuse why the child is not held to the same standards in history, science, and other subjects.

I feel that general knowledge is of the utmost importance and that it gets washed away in the IEP. I am fearful that the IEP has created a protective coating that gives the educators plenty of leeway to modify curriculum so simple that it takes all of the effort out of learning. Simply put, Jamie had gotten use to schoolwork being "easy" and failed to learn how to apply himself. Yes, his grades were A's all the time, but was he really learning? And had expectations fallen so low that he appeared to be, and saw himself, as a huge academic success?

The opposite was true. He wasn't, by any means.

The IEP simply needs to challenge the child. Expectations cannot be lowered, and motivation has to remain intact. These kids need to be challenged to higher standards. To hand out A's in order to nurture the child's self-esteem and relieve the teachers of parental pushback is very detrimental to the child. The IEP should be a plan that encompasses specific, relevant material to be taught on a daily basis.

As an example, Jamie's biggest struggle has been reading comprehension. I find that daily goals, including a large variety of information in the interest of science or history, would be much more valuable than some obscure, measurable reading goal.

In American history, if I were homeschooling Jamie, I would have a daily goal such as naming three causes of the "Great Depression." I would explain the reasons in detail to him, use graphics, have him write a paragraph about it, and then have him verbalize it to me. This would accomplish reading, comprehension, writing, spelling, and general knowledge goals. It is a small pearl, not a big chunk of information, but attainable; and at the end of the day the kid has something under his belt.

The same could be done in biology. Perhaps one day's goal could be naming the main differences between a plant and animal cell. Jamie could visualize the differences using a microscope, read about it in the text, and draw or make a model of the cells.

To set this style of learning in motion, a couple of big things would have to happen. First, these kids would have to have their own personal teacher assistant (paraprofessional). Secondly, these teacher assistants would have to communicate with the main teacher and plan out the daily goals, ascertaining the most important details of the day's lesson. When I homeschooled, I awoke a little earlier, prayed, drank my coffee, and planned the day's goals all in thirty minutes. I don't think It would be terribly time consuming. I don't think it should be.

I am optimistic that we have the means to help these children. Perhaps some financial responsibility and streamlining should be considered rather than the old-fashioned tax hike to afford such direct instruction. I am no expert in the Department of Education nor its budget at the federal, state, or local level, but I am led to believe that there is an enormous amount of money at their disposal. In my community, property values have nearly doubled in the last ten years, of course that spells higher property taxes, but our teachers here are starving. Surely the expense of bureaucracy is underrated. As with a bucket that has a hole, it is much more productive to repair the hole instead of pouring in endless amounts of water hoping to keep it full. In the deepest part of my being, I do not believe funding is the problem.

Through good schools void of the rigorous and useless standards, personalized education plans, and dedicated teachers, we can reach our kids. We can educate them, bringing them into a world full of wonder and enjoyment where they can find their place and contribute to society in a meaningful manner.

*Chapter Nine*

# The Right Stuff

*"Great things He hath taught us, great things He hath done, And great our rejoicing through Jesus the Son; But purer and higher, and greater will be, our wonder, our transport when Jesus we see."*

— *"To God Be the Glory," Fanny Crosby (1875)*

One of the main reasons I felt compelled to write this book is to share how God restored me, my son, and my family. I also want to share the good stuff—the right stuff that made a big difference in Jamie's life.

My intention is not to simply share a blog about the trials and tribulations of autism, but to proclaim the power, might, and goodness of our God. His goodness shines through when believers turn to Him in prayer and bold faithfulness. This book can't possibly be long enough to describe all of the mistakes I have made along the way, but I will share the few God-inspired interventions that collectively made a positive impact on my child with autism.

# Prayer

I realize that prayer has become more of something we say rather than something we do these days. And sad to say, it also tends to be the backup plan when all else fails. Why is that when it should be the first thing we do? This being said, I know for certain that prayers are powerful—the most powerful intervention of all.

My whole life is a testament to God's grace and the power of prayer. No, not all of my prayers have been answered in the way I asked, and God's timetable has certainly been different than mine. However, it is so amazing when He speaks.

Beau and I have both prayed over and with Jamie his whole life. Of course, we have prayed over Lisbeth and Drew as well. There have been incredible times when very specific prayers have been answered. There have also been times when our faith has lapsed and we wondered if it was even effective at all. (I hate how quickly we forget God's goodness.) But it is very powerful when done in a manner of blind faith.

One of my favorite verses, Philippians 4:6-7 reads, "Do not be anxious about anything, but in every situation, by prayer and petition with thanksgiving, present your requests to God." I love this verse and take it to mean that we can pray boldly, thanking God for what we have asked for in advance. I have many testimonies about praying boldly in this manner. One time that is prevalent on my mind is when Beau's ninety-two-year-old grandfather was diagnosed with a malignant tumor in his colon. Not a fan of chemotherapy or radiation, especially on a feeble elderly man, I prayed for the surgeon to remove the tumor and there be no residual cancer to treat. When I prayed earnestly for this beloved man, I knew God had answered. When the phone call came that he was free and clear of cancer, I was not surprised. I expected that result and praised God for it.

I have prayed for my marriage, and in times when communication was ineffective, I went straight to the top of the hierarchy. I asked God for what I needed from my husband. The Lord has restored my marriage on many occasions, in fact exactly as many times as I have asked Him. He has softened my heart, softened my husband's heart, and diffused so many meaningless spats.

Financially, we have both put our faith wholeheartedly in the Lord. And though we are far from wealthy people, we always seem to have "just enough." Beau and I know that He provides for our family, always has and always will.

I remember one season when we were financially strapped. The wolf came knocking at the door, and Beau was pretty stressed out. I actually remember praying for a lump sum of money. I knew if we could pay some things off, life would be easier. I actually thanked God for delivering it after I prayed because I knew it was coming. By that evening, we had it. Beau received an unexpected bonus from work. I had never prayed for money before, nor have I since that day.

We are also blessed to have a family that continually prays for our son. Beau's father prays specifically for Jamie every morning. Also, Beau's mother and her Sunday school group, belonging to the First Baptist Church of Lafayette, have earnestly prayed for Jamie over the years. They prayed for him when we were searching for just the right high school. They prayed for him to pass the driving test, to do well on exams, and in many more situations.

Well, Jamie miraculously got in to one of the best high schools around. He also passed his written driving test, and he even made the honor roll during ninth grade. The bible says in James 5:16, "The prayer of a righteous person is powerful and effective." I am so very grateful for these ladies and their faithful prayers.

My dad continually marvels at our three children. He says he can't get over how good-natured, generous, and kind they are to everyone they meet. I don't think I have to mention that my children are not perfect and not without fault, but they have made a significant impression on him. The funny thing is that he thinks that Beau and I have had something to do with it. He often remarks, "Something good is going on over at your house. You two must be great parents."

I always feel compelled to correct him after I get through a good laugh. I answer, "Dad, we are not great parents. Though we love them like crazy and try very hard, we make mistakes all the time." I continue pleading with him to understand, "Dad, I pray for my children. Sometimes several times a day."

Looking perplexed he asks, "With them or over them?"

Smiling, I answer, "All of the above."

My father is a precious Christian man with a huge heart for Jesus. I just feel that sometimes as believers, we fail to understand the great power unleashed through prayer. I know that this is true of me on many occasions. I am reminded of many disastrous mistakes I have made as a parent. Truly, I have felt like the world's worst. But in prayer, I lament to my heavenly Father asking Him for help, guidance, and wisdom. There has never been one time in the history of my life as a mom that He has failed to rescue me from my errors.

The formula to raising great kids, if there is one, is to: love the Lord with all your heart and soul, love each other deeply, and never cease praying like a warrior. The power is in Him.

Much of my story has been about responses to prayer. But truthfully, prayers are not always answered in the way we ask for them. In a world where free-will and natural consequences govern, it's so hard to try to understand God's role in it all. I have just stopped trying to understand it, and instead spend my time trying to comprehend how much He loves us. What I believe wholeheartedly is that praying petitions God to intervene. No matter what the outcome may be, it will always be optimal if our loving Father has anything to do with it. It is never a wasted effort, and in the presence of faith, He always responds.

Pray for your child. If you have a crisis of faith, then have a circle of believers pray for him/her. It is, by far, the best and most effective thing you can do.

## Diet

Diet has indeed played an important role in Jamie's progression. Keeping him off of highly processed and sugary foods has been a big help to his recovery. Of course, every family has to do what they can afford as far as time and money. I try to keep his diet limited to meats, fruits, vegetables, organic grains and dairy.

Many of the early years were spent on special diets and treating food allergies. In the beginning, I kept a food diary identifying what foods were tolerated and which weren't. This food diary definitely beats the expensive allergy tests in my opinion. I still refrain from buying anything in a box. Juices and fast food should also be avoided. For children with gastrointestinal issues, healthy dietary changes can significantly help with behavior. It should be one of the first interventions considered. I highly recommend homemade yogurt cultured for twenty-four hours for kiddos with tummy trouble (See Appendix for recipe). This special yogurt is very healing and probably better than any probiotic money can buy. I first learned of this magical and delicious treat from Elaine Gottschall's book, *Breaking the Vicious Cycle* regarding the Specific Carbohydrate Diet.[1] I found, in my own experience, that diet is directly linked to behavior.

## Supplements

Along with diet, supplements can prove beneficial. Some of my all-time favorites are fish or flax oil, coconut oil, probiotics, magnesium and B vitamins (when tolerated). It is important to do your research and purchase only high-quality supplements. Also, I have learned to only try one each week so you can evaluate the supplements individually. I have been greatly aided by a licensed nutritionist in this area.

## Vaccinations

Vaccinations should be highly thought out and given in single dose vials, eliminating harmful preservatives whenever possible. Just be aware of what is being injected into your child's body. Be your child's advocate. I would suggest using keen discernment in this matter, making sure the vaccinations are few and far between, necessary, and safe. I don't believe my child could have recovered had I kept assaulting his immune system with the overwhelming amount and assortment of vaccinations recommended.

## Behavior

Regarding behavior and discipline, the "unconditional love" approach really turned my child around. In conjunction with all of the other interventions such as diet, supplements, and sensory work, I believe this can prove very effective, especially for a child labeled O.D.D. (Oppositional Defiant Disorder). The approach is to first set them up for success, then use mercy and encouragement liberally, taking every opportunity to praise.

I am also a huge fan of A.B.A. therapy, as long as the instructor is trained, committed, and invested wholeheartedly in the child. It is very valuable when taught to parents and utilized as a lifestyle.

## Sensory Diet

Jamie's overwhelming sensory system was the first layer we peeled. He was intolerant of loud or high-pitched noises, different textures, vestibular activities, as well as changes in environment. In the early years, Beau and I incorporated a sensory diet in Jamie's everyday life.

We made sure he had a swing set. I taught him to climb trees and ride a bike which utilizes much vestibular activity. He loved to pull his little brother, Drew, all around our cul de sac in the wagon. We figured that was meeting some sort of sensory need. We simply kept him active. After many lessons and attempts, my father finally taught him to swim, and then we couldn't get him out of the pool.

I made sure he had plenty of tactile stimulation as well. We played in the sandbox and made things out of playdough. The Wilbarger protocol (aka brushing) was the real game changer though. It really helped to calm him down.

Being one to cover his ears at loud noises, I found the courage to take him to the movies. It wasn't easy, and at first this required many walks to the bathroom and lots of treats. But after many moons, he was finally able to sit somewhat quietly. To this day, if he doesn't understand the movie or is not interested, he will simply take a walk. We know and understand this about him.

Changes in his environment were a huge challenge. He was completely freaked out by hearing a sound or seeing something that was out of its element. I imagine his world was a little like one of those exercises that asks you to circle the item that doesn't belong in the picture. Simply put, he couldn't handle a shoe in the bathtub. He could neither process nor tolerate it.

I was at my brother's house in Texas when Jamie was about seven and began playing a Ray Charles tune on the piano so he would sing it so adorably like he did at home. When he heard the first couple of notes, he dashed out of the house with his hands over his ears and ran down the street. I had to catch him, calm him down, and bring him back.

He also could not tolerate seeing a teacher from school at our home. When his teacher, Miss G., would come to the house to tutor him in reading, it truly disoriented him. He had known her for five years and adored her, but could not process her being at our house. The only thing I could do was talk about his feelings and prepare him for the event. I would specifically explain to him when she would arrive, coach him on a greeting, show him where they would work, what they would read, and what time she would leave. This really helped. Alerting him of the situation, giving him structure, and creating a visual picture beforehand was very effective. I think trying to understand how Jamie felt and talking about it with him really made a difference. I had to convince him that he was safe even when his environment changed or became unpredictable.

This sensory piece took a lot of time and patience to work through. Thankfully, he eventually learned to calm himself down and can now handle most stressful situations like a champ.

## Auditory Processing

This was a big one. Learning to hear words and quickly assign mental pictures to them was a huge breakthrough for our boy. It took many years, but with the help of a dedicated and wise speech pathologist, Jamie was able to understand language. Margo taught us to play games with Jamie that would facilitate word retrieval such as "Simon Says." I also invested in a wonderful computer game called *Earaerobics* where he would use the mouse to click on pictures, numbers, or letters as quickly as he could when they were called aloud.[2]

This auditory piece was huge as it facilitated his understanding of the world by improving his communication. I found that as his level of communication increased, his frustration decreased.

# Fostering a Hobby

Jamie had so few interests as a little boy. Beau and I spent most of our time trying to get him involved in enjoyable activities. For so long he just wouldn't bite. It seemed futile until one summer when Lisbeth bought a Wii with her birthday money. He suddenly became interested in the *Super Mario Brothers* game. This was not the hobby we had in mind, but for the first time ever he was actually interested in something. He loved it and played the game so much I had to eventually limit the time he spent on it.

Over time, he became extraordinarily proficient at the game. For years, he was obsessed with Mario and Luigi. When I bought him all of the action figures, he started playing for the first time. He was primarily reenacting scenes from the game, not necessarily using his imagination, still I was thrilled. I eventually bought all three of them the costumes so they could role play. Jamie was Luigi, Drew was Mario, and Lisbeth was Princess Peach. I loved that this was something he could play with his siblings. This also gave him something to talk with other kids about.

Thanks to my father, golf was another avenue in which we were able to get him participating in life. My father was an avid golfer and would take Jamie whenever he could, from about seven years old, to the driving range. He would talk about golf quite a bit, explaining the game as they watched the major tournaments together. It was obvious at this time that Jamie was not paying attention. He was totally in another world. But one Saturday afternoon, I took Jamie to a very relaxed driving range in Denver and bought him a small bucket of balls. He just swung away. I was thrilled that he actually spent twenty minutes completing a task. It was huge. He felt very proud of himself and even mimicked my dad when we got home by "taking a shower after playing golf." It was absolutely precious. For many years I would take him to hit a small bucket of balls. I'm convinced he was trying to imitate my dad, his role model whom he idolized.

It took many years before he was even close to receiving instruction on his swing, but during the summer before sixth grade he started private golf lessons. The instructor, Matt, was patient, kind, and gave Jamie visuals as he worked with him. He was also careful to work on one concept at a time. This guy was priceless. Thanks to Matt and my father, Jamie started to hit the ball well enough to play on the course. I continue to take him to play nine holes every Saturday that I can.

Camping was another way we encouraged Jamie to enjoy life. We were able to teach Jamie how to set up a tent, build a fire, and most importantly— to roast smores and hot dogs. He loved it, and we loved the freedom of being outdoors without the constant snarl of society breathing down our necks. Jamie was blissfully calm and happy when we were in the beautiful outdoors. To this day, he is still a "happy camper."

Our little boy who did nothing but play "garage door," who could not enjoy playing or interacting with others, and who had no interests in anything, now has a life. Jamie now has many more interests such as crabbing and fishing with his Paw Paw in Louisiana, swimming, riding his bike, and playing the piano.

We never gave up trying to find something that he would enjoy. Hobbies are important to our kids on the spectrum. They give kids a sense of identity, goals, and the opportunity to come out of their world and reach other people.

# Family

God blessed Beau and I both with the best parents in the world. They loved us all with a passion and supported us anyway they possibly could. Each one of our parents brought something to the table that enriched Jamie's life. They also helped us with the other two who needed just as much time and attention. Beau and I had a hard road raising all three children in such difficult circumstances being so far away from everyone we had ever known. I honestly don't know what we would have done without our wonderful parents who always showed up. Their support was unfailing.

As the children got older, our parents took each one of the kids, individually, for a week or so every summer to spend valuable time with them. Their loving influence was crucial to the development of all of our children—but especially Jamie. Gran, Nana, Paw Paw and Popee, were definitely a big part of helping Jamie to overcome some of autism's most difficult challenges.

Jamie's siblings also made a huge difference in his life. He learned so much just by watching them and listening to them. On many occasions they included him in their activities, and by doing so, they brought him out of his lonely world. Though they could get aggravated with him at times, they were actually the best therapy of all.

I pray earnestly that other families would have the blessing of a support system whether it be family, friends, church, or the autism community. Families like mine need more help than we could ever admit. I know in the deepest part of my heart that our family's loving support made a huge impact on Jamie's recovery.

# Reading

By the time Jamie was in the fifth grade, he was still barely reading. I honestly didn't know if he would ever be able to read independently. He knew phonics well and could sound out words. He could also recognize many words by sight, but he just couldn't put it all together. He didn't "get it" at all. He struggled so hard to read most of the time that he would lose all comprehension. There was no enjoyment, no reward, and no gain. So, I listened to my friend Miss G., and started reading to him.

Every night for about two years, I read Jamie a chapter in a high interest book that I had carefully selected. I started off with books that had been made into a movie. I figured if he heard the story told in auditory form and then was able to see it take life in a visual form, he might become interested.

I actually had to mandate this reading time. He didn't want any part of it. I simply told him that he had no choice. This is what we were going to do. It didn't take long before he looked forward to crawling in my bed at night and listening. After each chapter, I would ask him questions about what I had read. He became better and better about answering the questions. His listening skills and comprehension progressed, and he ended up loving the stories. It was so rewarding to have a rich topic of conversation with this child who so often perseverated on mindless things. Now we had cool stories and characters to talk about. Now he enjoyed movies because he actually understood them.

We started off with *Because of Winn Dixie*,[3] next was *The Indian and the Cupboard*[4] and then, *The Lion, the Witch, and the Wardrobe*.[5] Eventually we started reading books that did not have a movie to accompany them, and he enjoyed them just as well. I felt that this story time was stimulating his brain, bringing new ideas into focus, and facilitating new conversation. I read sixteen books to this child, one chapter at a time. It proved to be one of the best interventions of all.

# Education

There is no doubt that homeschooling made a huge difference in Jamie's life. It gave him the one-on-one instruction he needed to learn foundational information. It also gave him confidence to perform as the environment was calm and non-threatening. I still advocate for and believe in great schools with great teachers presenting rich and interesting subject matter. I believe these schools should provide a liberal amount of direct instruction in an environment of care and compassion. But until this becomes a reality, homeschooling is a great option.

Though my child greatly benefited from the two years he was homeschooled, it was more of an emergency short-term intervention that had a means to an end. My opinion stands that homeschooling is most remarkable and successful when adopted as a lifestyle. With committed parents and community involvement from kindergarten to 12$^{th}$ grade, there can be no greater advantage. With the resources available, children have plenty of opportunity to socialize in co-op environments, play sports, enter science fairs... and participate in local missions.

In my community, the opportunities are endless for the homeschooled child. I truly wish that I had learned about this beautiful way of life before my children started school. But, my choices were made long ago. They are all public-school children and that's perfectly fine. They are all doing beautifully to this day. It is possible that God wants them to shine their light there where they can make a difference. We are told in the Bible by Jesus, "Neither do people light a lamp and put it under a bowl. Instead they put it on its stand, and it gives light to everyone in the house. In the same way, let your light shine before others that they may see your good deeds and glorify your Father in heaven" (Matthew 5:16).

Homeschooling is a big commitment and a tremendous labor of love. If you can do it, and God calls you to it, I highly recommend it. Kiddos like Jamie need a lot of attention and one-on-one, especially in the early years. I have listed ten things that I found crucial to homeschooling. As I dove into the homeschool world and journaled, I look back and see how I was transformed by the experience. As a result, I have put together some valuable suggestions that I learned along the way for any parent desiring to embark on this journey. Here is my personal homeschool handbook:

## #1 Clean Out Your Closet

I love the movie "War Room."[6] One of my favorite scenes is when Pricilla Shirer cleans out her closet to prepare room for God to do His work. I had to clean out my own figurative closet by confessing my sins and getting rid of my negative, unhealthy attitudes. If in doubt, throw it out. God won't compete with all of our junk.

## #2 Surrender Completely

Surrender yourself and surrender your child. Accept God's will for your child. Make sure you differentiate your earthly desires for your child from God's heavenly ones. When it comes down to it, do we really treasure the typical success driven, materialistic, self-absorbed life? Want more? Strive high but share in God's plan for your child. For His plan far outshines yours, I promise.

## #3 Become an Expert on Unconditional Love

Have clear expectations and goals but offer mercy generously.

## #4 Pray Without Ceasing

I pray in the shower, brushing my teeth, washing dishes and while driving. This helps me keep God in my perspective. He offers hope and life. He also gives so many great ideas and solutions.

During the homeschool years, He was my greatest resource. He truly inspired many of the great ideas I had in teaching difficult material. I would pray and the ideas would flood my mind. Proverbs 3:6 reads, "In all your ways submit to him, and he will make your paths straight."

## #5 K.I.S.S.

Keep It Simple Sam. Have a goal in sight. Meet your child exactly where he/she is at, not where you think they should be. Be careful not to overcomplicate education. Formulate a hierarchy of subjects, deciding which is the most important and work from there. It is best to stay practical.

When I was at my wits end, not knowing exactly what was most important to teach Jamie (there was just so much he needed to learn), I decided to start with one thing. I would prioritize teaching him the Bible. He may not learn anything else from me, but he would know Jesus. I came to understand that this was the best place to start. It gave him a sense of purpose and an origin to cling to. The Word of God certainly gives us all an identity.

I used a very easy to read paraphrased Living Bible. It was amazing how well he read this text. It was like he struggled reading everything else, but this Living Bible he read with ease. We started with the Gospels.

## #6 Use Direct Instruction

There is no substitute for it. My child had severe issues with reading. He wasted six years in a special needs classroom because of low expectations. At this point time was not on our side. Instruction with children that struggle has to be specific, and the evaluation of the success has to be immediate. With direct instruction, you can assure that they have grasped the material before moving on.

My good friend, who is a teacher, asked me once when I was homeschooling, "Do you grade his spelling tests?"

I said "Yes! And he always makes 100%." I then explained to her that I keep testing and working with him until he has mastered 100% of the material. That is the beauty of immediate evaluation. Independent work can be for practicing mastered skills. This too is important. I believe one-on-one direct instruction for a period of time is well worth the sacrifice.

## #7 Teach About Life

Beau and I taught Jamie to ice skate, snow ski, grocery shop, count money, cook, drive a car, and much more through the years. My father taught him to swim, and my father-in-law taught him to fish. His world could not be limited to academics. Our most important goal for him was to be independent and self-sufficient. Homeschooling allowed me more time to teach him some much-needed life skills.

Take every opportunity to teach your child everything you can. Life itself is quite an education.

## #8 Get a Life of Your Own

I would get stuck in teaching mode, driving my kids crazy. Taking every opportunity to make every moment a learning experience should be applauded. However, I have found it's good to give it a rest every now and then.

I learned to just let the kids veg out sometimes. I also started trying to make time away from home with my husband and friends. It's not quite healthy to be in teaching mode 24/7. Our lives need balance.

## #9 Plan on Getting Discouraged or Depressed

There is absolutely no way around this. Homeschooling is a monumental task. It really helps to know this will happen so you can have a plan of attack ready.

There were many dark days when I felt like a complete failure. I found myself getting impatient, raising my voice, or just going off to cry it out. When you are lost in the weeds and can't see where you are going, sometimes it's best to just sit down and have a picnic. You are entitled to enjoy your life along the journey, and so is your child

On these days, I learned to just close the book and switch to something fun. I usually called it a day when either one of us would get frustrated or sad. Jamie and I would go out to lunch, to a movie or sometimes take a nice, long walk. I always tried to make sure the day ended on a good note. When the heart or attitude is not right, pushing is futile and I would even say harmful to the relationship. The heart and spirit of the child and the weary parent must be nurtured from time to time.

#10 Praise! Praise! Praise!

Take every opportunity to praise your child for every success, no matter how small. It is the ultimate tactic—the best motivator of all. They absolutely live for this.

Also, give due praise and thanks to our Lord. He will do miraculous things for you and your child when you walk with Him. These "little miracles," I like to call them, are quite inconspicuous. It is important to be aware and notice them.

Make sure your child sees every success as a step closer to their goal. Make their accomplishments relevant to the goal in sight whether it be college, vocational school, or landing a job at *Home Depot.* My dear friend and Jamie's beloved tutor, Jeffrey Freed has taught me this valuable pearl of wisdom. He advises in his book *Right-Brained Children in a Left-Brained World,* "The right-brained child will work harder in his studies if he understands that school can help him reach a goal."[7]

# What Does Healing Look Like?

To say a word about healing— yes, I absolutely believe that God will heal our children. (I sincerely believe that he has healed mine.) However, He will heal according to His divine purposes. He will heal to the extent that He alone defines. It will look different for every family and every child.

When Jamie was in second grade, I did some research on homeopathy. Honestly, it sounded a little creepy and strange, but I had read that many people have had a great deal of success with it. I figured, who am I to limit the way God heals? To me, anything that was not blasphemy was fair game.

At the first homeopathy appointment, I was quite skeptical and uneasy. The walls were painted a strange pale pink in the office. The place had a funny smell and an unusual vibe which was neither good nor bad. As I nervously followed Jamie around trying to prevent a meltdown or the destruction of property, I asked the sweet-natured receptionist a not-so-profound question. I asked, "Does this stuff really work?" I expected she would answer me because not many people would be so bold as to ask this million-dollar question.

She did answer and was very careful with her words. She carefully said, "Yes, I have seen it work. It depends on the situation but..." (This was the part she offered with caution.) "it doesn't always work the way you think it's going to work."

I thought, "What in the world does she mean by that?"

Over the years, I have pondered over those words many times. It's now almost ten years later, and I think I now understand what she meant. Jamie received a regular homeopathic remedy for about one year, and during the course of the treatment he changed. We did not see it as a good change. In fact, I was scolded by my mother and got a few harsh comments from teachers at school who couldn't help but notice.

What happened was that my sweet little boy who rarely made eye contact, had very little interest in playing with anyone or anything, who mostly stimmed with his "Handy Dandy Notebook" or makeshift garage door, became hyper, mischievous, and at times, maniacal.

All exaggeration aside, during the course of treatment, Jamie's behavior became horrible. He would run around saying potty words laughing hysterically. He would break his siblings' toys and laugh when they cried. He would attempt to flush big rocks down the toilet, throw things at the neighbor's dog, say cuss words, and yell out inappropriately in school and in public.

I wasn't so sure I hadn't poisoned him. But looking back now, I can see that he was provoking a response from everyone around him. He had woken up and wanted to participate in life but didn't quite know how. He was in a fog before. He rarely looked when I called his name and did not even seem to notice others. Now he was boisterous and obnoxious, making sure everyone on the planet knew he existed. Was this actually a path to healing? Was it just an alternate path, or was it merely a predictable progression of autism or a developmental stage? These are questions I will not even pretend to know the answer to. I will only ask, "What if God works in this manner?" Is it possible that He heals us, not in the manner in which we think He will, but in that which He knows we need?

There was no straight path to the top with my son. It feels like we have been to the tumultuous ends of the earth and back with him. We have fought, cried, pleaded, and tried to buy every service on this earth to help him. It has been a struggle that few people can identify with. But what if the Maker used this anguish to mold Beau and I, making us into something better? What if all of this hardship was the infamous "Refiner's Fire" mentioned in 1 Peter 1:7. So I ask again, "What if God's plan for us is different than we think it should be?" Is it still not a plan—a plan from the Creator of the universe that loves us more than we can even fathom?

I believe from the bottom of my heart and soul that the answer is yes. God is always working in our favor. He is never the cause of pain and suffering but instead our relief, our remedy, and I say, "Who are we to question." For His end game is always what we need.

# Recovery

I like using the term "recovered" when describing where Jamie is now. I consider recovery as the relief of the debilitating symptoms of autism, and I believe Jamie has come through.

According to the Diagnostic and Statistical Manual of Mental Disorders-Fourth Edition (DSM-IV), the main diagnostic reference of mental health professionals, autism is identified through three main areas. They are: impairment in social interaction, impairments in communication, and restricted, repetitive and stereotyped patterns of behavior, interests, and activities.[8] Each one of these areas is described with specific detail, a checklist more or less. As I revisit these diagnostic criteria, I do not need to pay several hundreds of dollars for an expert, who knows much less about autism than I do, to tell me that my son has very few of the markers left.

In evaluating social interaction, I would say Jamie is practically neurotypical. He makes eye contact routinely with everyone he speaks to, holding out his hand while making proper introductions. He can converse with others about their interests and is more than willing to participate in unfamiliar activities in order to have social significance.

He seeks out social opportunities and tries to conform to the culture in any way he can without compromising his intrinsic values. He has many friends and thoroughly enjoys connecting with everyone using his social media. As well, he has learned not to engage with those who seek to humiliate and tease him or with those who show problematic lifestyles. In short, he makes friends easily with those who share his own values. Not only is he creating friendships, he is choosing nice kids to associate with.

During his freshman year, Jamie came home from Christmas break with a very special card including a gift certificate to Chick-Fil-A. A sweet young girl in one of his classes wrote him a tender card thanking him for going out of his way to tell her hello every single day and asking how she was. This girl explained that she did not have many people to talk to and that he brightened her days. This might be the one thing that makes me the proudest of my son. Without a doubt, he has social skills. They are very simple but profound, positively impacting the lives of others.

Jamie attends church youth group on Sunday nights with marked enthusiasm. He mingles, participates in the activities, and really enjoys worship. He even attended camp this past summer, being independent and on his own for the first time. He attends many of the school football games and functions. He is on the school newspaper and does his very best to capture interviews and stories. He meets up with friends at the rec. center or at the golf course and always manages to have someone to hang out with.

I will admit his interactions can seem a little awkward, and his conversation can be a little stale at times, but he is present, in the moment, interacting with people. It is true that some kids blow him off as an annoyance, but many truly enjoy being around him and appreciate the honesty and sincerity he brings to the table. As well as social reciprocity, he also demonstrates deep empathy for others, in fact it is one of his best qualities.

He calls and consoles a friend whose girlfriend just broke up with him, or calls to congratulate a friend who just became an uncle. He also frequently calls and checks on my sick aunt as well as our ninety-two-year-old grandfather. He continually displays a ton of compassion for the sick and the brokenhearted.

In the area of communication, he is making progress daily. I find his vocabulary to be a bit limited, but Jamie can certainly communicate all of his thoughts, feelings, and needs without any difficulty. He has no trouble expressing himself, and in his own way, void of capricious babbling and fancy jargon, does so quite effectively.

Jamie is also now starting to understand idioms and figurative language. He can also read my facial expressions to tell if I am joking or being serious. He can even catch onto a joke and play along with it.

His communication skills, though possibly a tad behind, are constantly improving. He is now capable of having a conversation on a topic of someone else's interest, asking questions while remaining attentive. He is also starting to understand sarcasm and even use it; Lord help me.

The restrictive and stereotypical behaviors have all but disappeared. Knowing very well that they function to calm an individual on the spectrum down from being overstimulated, I'm pretty sure Jamie has just developed more discreet ways to accomplish this. For instance, he needs time to go down into his basement room to decompress after a long day at school. I don't see any repetitive movements or unusual habits, but his schedule and routine serve to keep him calm and tranquil. However, a disruption in his routine is now handled beautifully, no doubt with lots of effort on his part. I can't remember the last time I have seen a true meltdown from Jamie. As he has learned to self-regulate, they are a rare occurrence.

Jamie can still perseverate on a few topics every now and then, and I don't know if that goes in the social or language column. Though it is definitely fading, this is one of the things that we are still working on. This has been a big obstacle over the years. In the past, it would often be extremely annoying catch phrases that he would repeat over and over in an attempt to gain a response. In fact, I got so tired of hearing my own voice nagging him, "say it once" that I started using hand gestures to alert him to knock it off. I showed him what it meant, and with the wiggle of my hand he would stop.

Today, it is just topics of conversations from time to time that I have to intervene upon. I usually say, "We've already talked about this. Let's talk about something new." Everyday it's less and less that I am compelled to remind him as his conversations have become more diverse and interesting. I have come to look forward to our time each day in the car when we share meaningful discussions.

Perhaps there is no cure within the autism spectrum, but this is not what I seek. What I do believe in wholeheartedly is the concept of recovery. My son has, by leaps and bounds, recovered by overcoming the incapacitating symptoms that once threatened to diminish his life.

Jamie still struggles, and it's possible he always will. He still has so much to learn, especially about interacting with his peers. He still makes a ton of mistakes in social situations, but each one serves as a valuable teaching moment. I am grateful that, even throughout the most embarrassing times, he is willing and able to learn. I am also thankful for the quality of life and the growth we see from him every single day. I am convinced that God healed our son. I am convinced that He did it His way, and more impressive, He did it in spite of my own efforts. And to take it a step further, He healed me in the process. He healed me from myself. He saved me from the likeness of self-pity, despair, and sadness. He rescued me from the root of bitterness fostered by unforgiveness, anger, and resentment. He did it His way, and I don't regret a minute of the pain because it has brought me closer to Him.

*Chapter Ten*
# The Potter

*"Mold me and make me after Thy will, while I am waiting yielded and still"*

— *"Have Thine Own Way," Adelaide Pollard (1907)*

I wish I had a nickel for every message I have heard at church about Jesus' "Prodigal Son" parable (Luke 15:11-32). It is probably the most well-known and well combed over parable in the Bible. Still I have this nagging sense that there is something much more significant to the story that we seldom recognize.

In this story we have a rebellious sinner who loses his way and abandons his Father. We then have reconciliation and forgiveness. Next, we have jealousy and resentment from the loyal brother who never leaves his Father's side. But I don't see either of the two brothers or their actions as the main crux of the story. I believe it's all about the Father. When the prodigal returns, we find the Father outside watching and waiting as it reads, "But while he was still a long way off, his Father saw him and was filled with compassion…" (Luke 15:20). Perhaps he stood outside every single day that his son was gone— looking, searching, reaching, longing. This part of the story always brings tears to my eyes. I feel that the Father's unwavering love for his children is the message.

My story is a bit of the same. It is not about me—what I did right, what I did wrong, how people treated me, how I reacted. It's not actually about the clay. It's about the Potter. Mine is a story about our heavenly Father's love. Although I may wander astray, far from my Father's house at times, I know that He watches and waits for me, and He continues to be filled with compassion for me, for all of us.

He molded me and changed me. He transformed me through every struggle and though every victory. He certainly transformed me through grief. The closeness I felt with the Creator of the universe when our baby died is an experience I will never forget. About twice a year I pull down my memory box where Amelia's blanket is along with her footprints and a single rose that lay on her casket. It does me good to cry for a bit and remember her. I continue to draw on these painful memories in order to be reminded of the vast love the Lord has for me. I am also reminded of the special dream. I must never forget that He gave me three times what I asked Him for when He blessed us with Jamie, Lisbeth, and Drew.

Through periods of incapacitating fear and anxiety, He has strengthened my faith. I've learned to cast my troubles on Him. I am not expected to save the world, only to remain obedient. I can retire my superhero cape and know that things beyond my control belong to him. Though my anxiety continues to rear its ugly head from time to time, I realize that our battles are never over as long as the enemy remains. However, reading the Bible and claiming God's promises keep my fears at bay. Praise and worship also help me to keep things in perspective.

The sadness I experienced after Jamie was diagnosed with autism was instrumental in shaping my character. Going through this devastating period of sadness has allowed me to feel a deeper sense of joy. As gratefulness now thrives in my heart, I have hope and peace to cling to when life is disappointing. As dear old Bob Ross, the inspiring painter and host of "The Joy of Painting" on PBS, would say as he would contrast a landscape, "You have to have dark in order to have light."[1]

To abate the anger and resentment that tainted my loving heart for so long, I am learning to set healthy boundaries. I am no longer afraid of the resistance that I continue to encounter from time to time. Living with a loving and peaceful heart is so worth the temporary discomfort that setting boundaries can bring. The Holy Spirit convicts me that I am responsible for my own happiness. It is also my personal duty to refuse to be the subject of condemnation and criticism. I have to purposefully choose each day to live "not easily offended." It is in this capacity that I can serve to my fullest potential, glorifying the Lord.

Through His Word, I have learned that forgiveness is a way of life. We all need grace, and to withhold it from others when God generously offers it to us, brings death and destruction to our character. Learning the art of forgiveness has certainly changed my life. It rescued me from the "great madness" and helped me to love and live again. I will always pray for Immaculee and know that our compassion for others must never be superseded by our own needs and desires. I will continue to practice compassion by faithfully praying for others. Besides the fact that it brings me joy, I never again want to lose my ability to forgive. I want to live freely immersed in mercy and forgiveness, not only because of my own sinful nature but because I love Jesus. He is my ultimate motivation.

When my journey began, I could not possibly fathom the depths of love the Potter had for me, nor the plan He had in mind to mold me and make me into something worthwhile. Through all of the fear, pain, suffering, and discouragement, He had a plan. It was not the plan I wanted or hoped for. It was His plan, and it was so much more than anything I could have ever imagined.

Sometimes when I look into the sweet and tender blue eyes of my son with autism, I truly feel sorry for the rest of the world. What a blessing and a gift he is. He brings me pure joy every single day, and I love watching him enjoy life to the fullest.

I look at my sweet daughter Lisbeth in awe at the incredible person she has become and the strong constitution she has received in response to earnest prayer. The obstacles that she has overcome in her life, no one could fathom. Under that delicate and gentle veneer, is a very convicted young lady who wavers not in the truth she knows about herself, her faith, or the world.

My youngest, Drew, is head strong, determined and such a hard worker, and I couldn't be prouder. His attributes are remarkable, but most of all I love his heart. He is quick to love, quick to forgive, and he overflows with compassion.

Beau has been better to me than I have ever deserved. It is true many times we both missed the mark; sometimes I was just hard to love. As the Lord put it on my heart during the darkest time in our marriage, He gave to me a faithful husband that would never leave me or give up on me under any circumstances. We have been married for nineteen years as of now. We are both so grateful to the

Lord for carrying us through such difficult times. Looking back at the hardships we faced, we feel that it is a miracle our marriage is now not only surviving but actually thriving.

The gratitude I feel towards my family cannot be expressed in words. My parents, as well as Beau's have loved and supported us through it all. They have helped us during hard times and given joyfully of their time and resources. Their dedication and love has been a gift, and we thank God for all of them.

What did I ever do to deserve such a blessed life? The answer is—absolutely nothing. I certainly don't deserve anything that is good, but in my better moments, I laid down my sword in surrender and humbly knelt and said, "Yes Lord." In surrender, and only through blind obedience was the Lord able to bless me. For nothing I have done in this life is good. The only good that comes from me is when I let my Lord sanctify and move through me.

Still there are questions that remain. I don't know why my beloved Amelia died in utero. I don't know why we were blessed over a year later with a beautiful child who has suffered with a most heart-wrenching disability. I don't know why my family had to endure such pain and difficulty. But what I do know is that I am so very grateful for my Lord and Savior. He loves me enough to refine and redefine my soul through it all. My life is full of joy, love, and laughter. I now live with a sense of gratefulness that I would have never been able to enjoy without the provision of my heavenly Father.

I feel that pain is necessary for change and growth, but God does not cause tragedy. Natural consequences and attacks from the enemy will continue to plague us as long as we live with free will. Instead, I know from both faith and experience that "God works for the good of those who love him, who have been called according to his purpose" (Romans 8:28). He is not the cause but the remedy to all suffering. I know that God loves us through our pain and has great empathy for us. I was made well aware of that in the dream I had after Amelia died. I also know that He strengthens us despite our pain and weakness. In fact, the bible actually tells us that His power "is made perfect in weakness" (2 Corinthians 12:9).

I know that many times I have fallen, and to this day continue to fail from time to time. Those who know me best know that being "yielded and still" is quite a challenge for me. But in my life, Jesus is always there to rescue, forgive, and transform my heart. God knows my heart and certainly knows the sin there within. Still, He loves me enough to stop each time to mold me and make me something better than before. I am convinced of His transforming power over my life. I am living proof of the growth.

I am now certain of three things: bad things will happen to me, people will continue to hurt and disappoint me, and last but most important, God will never leave me and will stand by me through the fire. Though it is certain to be unpleasant, the fire does not last and only proves to refine my soul. God's infinite love for me, however, lasts for eternity.

# Epilogue

I pull up to Jamie's high school parking lot around 2:50 pm. I see him waving and smiling at me from twenty-five feet away. He is walking fast and can hardly contain the smile that is on his face. As he gets in the car and proceeds to tell me about his day, I know there is nothing extra special that happened. It was just another good day for my happy boy.

In anticipation, he begins to tell me all about his friends and the goings-on at lunch. He is perfectly honest about all of his classes and pending homework but can't wait to get through the academic drill to get to the social stuff. He is over the moon excited about asking a girl to the homecoming dance soon approaching. The facts are: he loves school, he has a ton of friends, and loves the whole experience. It is surreal, and I must pinch myself to make sure it is not all just a lovely dream.

At the completion of this book, Jamie is in the tenth grade. Most all of his schoolwork is still modified, but he continues to work extremely hard in his studies. He is surrounded by caring teachers and has a ton of friends. He is extremely social and is almost always appropriate in his actions and conversations as he is blessed with a positive school environment.

He is also a member of the golf team there. The kids have been accepting, and the coaches continue to be patient and kind. It has been a valuable experience for him to stay focused, execute his swing correctly, follow the rules, and keep score. He has managed beautifully, and though he did not make the varsity team, he is improving every day. With the progress he is demonstrating, I am hopeful he will make it by the time he is a senior.

He is successfully learning to drive with his learner's permit. By the time he is a junior, he should be independently driving himself to school each day. This independence is so very important to him that he has saved up well over a thousand dollars so far to buy his own car.

He also loves his family. Family means everything to Jamie. He still maintains very close bonds with every single one of his grandparents. He is particularly close to my father, and they visit on the phone or facetime almost every day. He is also faithful to call our granddaddy (Beau's ninety-two-year-old grandfather) and his Aunt Nellie every Friday.

Jamie never fails to say the most beautiful prayer of thanksgiving at our dinner table each night. You can hear him sing with all sincerity and enthusiasm during worship at our community church, his arms raised high displaying his most treasured WWJD bracelet. He cheerfully helps out around the house and is very close to his siblings. His heart is full of joy, and his actions everyday prove his love for Jesus.

Cleaning his room one day, I found a list of things he planned to do during the summer. On the list he included: going to the zoo, going on a picnic with friends, playing golf, going to Louisiana to visit grandparents, but amongst other activities listed was praying a lot and praising God. How many of us put praying and praising God on our "things to do" list? My boy is special alright!

This beautiful human being that God created is so pure; people actually flock to him wherever he goes. His honesty, integrity, and compassion are so attractive. Jamie, with what we all call a disability, actually has a gift. He is not out to impress. Brennan Manning in my favorite book, "Abba's Child," describes the "imposter" as a false self we create to gain acceptance and approval. Manning explains, "Living out of the false self creates a compulsive desire to present a perfect image to the public so that everybody will admire us and nobody will know us."[1] Jamie does not have to become the imposter. He does not have to hide in fear, shame or guilt, overridden by hurts from the world. He does not suffer from an identity crisis. Jamie takes God's word at face value and engraves it on his heart. He knows he is a valuable child for whom God sacrificed His only Son. He knows that God loves, forgives, heals, and will never abandon him. Jamie believes this wholeheartedly. In my eyes and in my heart, the battle has already been won. Everything else I would like to call "lagniappe," a well-known French word for "something extra, a bonus, a gift."

I don't know what Jamie's future will hold. I don't know if he will attend college or trade school. What I do know is that he will have a beautiful life. He will be able to live independently, hold some sort of job that he performs with the utmost dedication, and maintain meaningful relationships.

What I also know is that there is nothing beyond Jamie's reach, and it has been my greatest pleasure in life watching God work through this young man's life. What a blessing and a privilege getting to be a part of it all!

I am overcome with joy to say that today my household of three teenagers, one mischievous dog, and a bearded dragon named "Rocky," is virtually no different than any other. Our struggles, our joys, our expectations, and our limitations are the same as any other family. We have all been through so much and have definitely lived through some of the darkest of hours, but here we survive with an outstanding resilience holding onto big hopes and dreams for the future.

As for me, I know it is time for a new chapter in my life—a new season. All three of my children will soon be graduating from high school, and my first task is almost complete. There is so much left for me to do. I know with the Holy Spirit guiding my life and permeating my thoughts, that I have just begun. My earnest desire is to give back to the Lord that has been so gracious to me. As I am learning to surrender on a minute by minute, daily basis, I will be able to enter this new season. I recognize that the Lord continues to condition me, train me, and teach me so that I may be in fighting shape to do His work. I recognize that it is time for a new song.

I was running one day, praying about His plans for my future when this song came to me. I hadn't heard it in decades and remembered most of the words to the first stanza. I sang it over and over again for months, played it on the piano, and even reinvented it with a more contemporary arrangement when I finally looked up all of the words. And the meaning in the lyrics to this beautiful hymn, *Take My Life and Let It Be*, I am convinced, is my future.

> *"Take my life and let it be, consecrated Lord to Thee*
>
> *Take my hands and let them move at the impulse of Thy love*
>
> *At the impulse of Thy love.*

*Take my feet and let them be, swift and beautiful for Thee*

*Take my voice and let me sing, always, only, for my King.*

*Always, only, for my King*

*Take my sliver and my gold, not a mite would I withhold.*

*Take my moments and my days, let them flow in endless praise.*

*Let them flow in endless praise.*

*Take my will and make it Thine, It shall be no longer mine.*

*Take my heart it is Thine Own. It shall be Thy royal throne,*

*It shall be Thy royal throne."*

— *"Take My Life and Let It Be,"*
*Frances Ridley Havergal (1874)*

Up until now I have given all of my time, energy, and resources to my own family. I feel sure that my time to serve is approaching. Perhaps He will call me to tutor local disadvantaged kids in math or reading. Maybe I will volunteer in the neighborhood schools helping children with learning differences learn to read or write. It is possible that He calls me to missionary work in desperate countries where I can serve with my nursing background. I don't know yet, and it doesn't really matter as long as I say yes. For I know as long as I obey, my life will be truly rewarding, abounding with peace and joy that can only come from serving the Lord Jesus.

My earnest desire is to give Him my life, my hands, my feet, voice, money, time, and most of all— my heart. As noble and righteous as this sounds, I know without a doubt that I will fail over and over again. In fact, at the completion of this work, I would still be considered for the "Least Likely to Write a Christian Book" award. But as Brennen Manning candidly responds in *The Ragamuffin Gospel*, "While Jesus calls each of us to a more perfect life, we cannot achieve it on our own. To be alive is to be broken; to be broken is to stand in the need of grace."[2]

I will always be eternally grateful for His Grace, and forever mindful that I will never cease being the clay in the Potter's hands.

# Appendix

## Further Reading

### Faith

Hayford, Jack, *I'll Hold You in Heaven*

Illibagiza, Immaculee, *Led by Faith*

Illibagiza, Immaculee, *Left to Tell*

Manning, Brennan, *Abba's Child: The Cry of the Heart for Intimate Belonging*

Manning, Brennan, *The Ragamuffin Gospel*

Tripp, Tedd, *Shepherding a Childs Heart*

### Autism/Health

Bock, Kenneth, *Healing the Childhood Diseases*

Dachel, Anne, *The Autism Cover-up*

Gardner, Nuala, *A Friend Like Henry: The Remarkable True Story of an Autistic Boy and the Dog That Unlocked His World*

Gottschall, Elaine Gloria, *Breaking the Vicious Cycle*

Habakus, Louise Kuo, *Vaccine Epidemic*

Kirby, David, *Evidence of Harm*

Maloney, Beth Alison, *Saving Sammy: A Mother's Fight to Cure Her Son's OCD*

Rubin, Jordan S., *The Maker's Diet*

Serroussi, Karen, *Autism and pervasive developmental disorders; A Mother's Story*

Stehli, Annabel, *The Sound of a Miracle*

## Education

Boyack, Connor, *Passion-Driven Education*

Cooper, Elaine, *When Children Love to Learn*

Coyle, Daniel, *The Talent Code*

Davis, Ronald D., *The Gift of Dyslexia*

Freed, Jeffrey, M.A.T. and Parsons, Laurie, *Right Brained Children in a Left Brained World*

Macaulay, Susan Schaeffer, *For the Children's Sake*

Robinson, Ken, Ph.D., and Aronica, Lou, *Creative schools*

Rose, Colin, *Accelerated Learning*

Weldon, Laura Grace, *Free Range Learning*

# Healing Yogurt

I am a firm believer that improved brain function comes from improved intestinal health. This very potent yogurt provides natural probiotics that safeguard the gut from harmful bacteria. I am quite certain that it brought my son, Jamie, out of a severe yeast/bacteria intoxication tremendously improving the quality of his life.

The 24-hour fermentation process breaks down the casein in the milk so even the most sensitive individual can tolerate this.

This Recipe for homemade yogurt is my version taken from Kendall Conrad's *"Eat Well Feel Well"*[1]

1-quart whole milk (organic)

1 quart half-and -half (organic)

2 packages (10 grams) Yogourmet starter.

You will need a yogurt maker and the yogurt starter packets. Both can be purchased on Amazon.

1. Bring the milk and half-and-half to a simmer in a large saucepan over medium heat stirring often.

2. Remove from heat and allow to cool to room temperature/ lukewarm. (This is a crucial step and may take a few hours.)
3. Once cool, strain the liquid through a wire mesh strainer into a pitcher that has been properly sterilized/cleaned.
4. Pour one cup of this liquid in a clean glass and add the two packets of yogurt starter whisking in both directions.
5. Add this cup back into the big pitcher with the rest and whisk again 10 times each way.

You are now ready to pour the yogurt into the glass containers that came with your machine. The dome can be placed on top and the machine can be turned on. Leave the yogurt heating for 24 hours. This is the time that the maximum amount of cultures can be obtained. Once the time is completed, cap the jars and refrigerate.

This yogurt is very potent, and you should start with 2 tablespoons initially. It is fantastic in smoothies and with fresh fruit such as peaches, strawberries and blueberries. It is best to sweeten with local honey as recommended.

# Notes

## Preface

1. Glorious is Thy Name, B.B. McKinney, copyright 1942.

## Chapter 1
## Our story

1. Joe. (MSC Nutrition), dietician. "MTHFR Mutation Symptoms and Diet: What you Need to Know." Diet vs Disease and MTHFR Mutation. November 30, 2017.
2. "Methyl-B12: A Treatment for ASD With Methylation Issues." Talk About Curing Autism. May 29, 2017 https://tacanow.org/family-resources/methylb12-a-treatment-for-asd-with-methylation-issues/

## Chapter 2
## Adventures in Autism

1. "ARI Moving Forward (2011)." Autism Research Institute. https://www.autism.com/ed_movingforward
2. Cave, Stephanie, MD, F.A.A.E.P., and Deborah Mitchell. *What Your Doctor May Not Tell You About Your Children's Vaccinations.* New York, NY: Grand Central Publishing, 2001.
3. Serroussi, Karen. *Autism and Pervasive Developmental Disorder: A Mother's Story of Research and Recovery.* NY: Simon and Schuster,2000.
4. Serroussi, Karen, *Autism and Pervasive Developmental Disorder,* 72-73

## Chapter 3
## New Beginnings and Bad Behaviors

1. "The Wilbarger Protocol (brushing therapy) for Sensory Integration," National Autism Resources, accessed May 14 2018, https://www. nationalautismresources.com/the-wilbarger-protocol-brushing-therapy-for-sensory-integrateion/
2. Gottschall, Elaine B.A., MSc. *Breaking the Vicious Cycle: Intestinal Health Through Diet*. Baltimore, Ontario, Canada: Kirkton Press, 1994.
3. Gardner, Nuala. *A Friend Like Henry*. Leicester: Charnwood, 2008.
4. Freed, Jeffrey, M.A.T., and Laurie Parsons. *Right-Brained Children in a Left-Brained World Unlocking the Potential of your ADD Child*. New York, NY: Simon and Schuster Paperbacks, 1997. 178-179
5. Robinson, Ken, Ph.D., and Lou Aronica. *Creative Schools*. New York, NY: Penguin Random House LLC, 2015.
6. Meme Heinenman, Viviana Gonzalez and Paula Chan, "What is ABA Therapy Now, Really?" Autism Support Network, 2016 https:// www. autismsupportnetwork.com/news/what-aba-now-really-autism-33299272.

## Chapter 4
## Hidden Blessings

1. Tripp, Tedd. *Shepherding a Child's Heart*. Second edition ed. Wapwallopen, PA: Shepherd Press, 2005

## Chapter 6
## Education: The Lifeline

1. Cherry, Ronald R. "American Judeo-Christian Values and the Declaration of Independence." Renew America, July 5, 2011, http://www. renewamerica.com/columns/cherry/110705.
2. Macaulay, Susan Schaeffer. *For the Children's Sake: Foundations for Home and School*. Wheaton, IL: Crossway Books, 1984, 43.
3. Boyack, Connor, and John Taylor Gatto. *Passion-driven Education: How to Use Your Childs Interests to Ignite a Lifelong Love of Learning*. Lehi, UT: Libertas Press, 2016.
4. Boyack and Gatto, *Passion-driven Education*, 40

5. "English Language Arts Standards, Writing, Introduction," Common Core State Standards Initiative, 2018, corestandards.org http://www.corestandards.org/ELA-literacy/W/introduction/

6. Weiss, Jeffrey. "Common Core Critics See Examples of Agenda in Class Assignments. *Dallas Morning News,* November 18, 2013. http://www.dallasnews.com/news/education/2013/11/18/common-core-critics-see-examples-of-agenda-in-class-assignments.

7. Proverbs 31: 10-31. NIV

8. Macaulay, *For the Children's Sake,* 5-7

9. Macaulay, *For the Children's Sake,* 148

10. Macaulay, *For the Children's Sake,* 28

11. Macaulay, *For the Children's Sake,*16

12. Macaulay, *For the Children's Sake,*

13. Winwood, Steve. "Roll with It" from the album "Roll with It" 1988, Virgin Records.

14. Davis, Ronald D., and Eldon M. Braun. *The Gift of Dyslexia.* New York, N.Y.: The Berkeley Publishing Group, 1994, 1997.
Revised Edition 1994 by the Ability Workshop Press

15. Wren, Sebastian, Ph.D. "Matthew Effects in Reading." Balancedreading.com. August 7, 2003. http://www.balancedreading.com/Matthew.html.

16. Freed and Parsons, *Right-Brained Children*

17. Freed and Parsons, *Right-Brained Children,* 53

18. Farmer, Letz. *Mastering Mathematics.* Arden, NC: Mastery Publications, 1988, 1990.

19. Davis and Braun, *The Gift of Dyslexia,* 113

# Chapter 7
# Hidden Sins

1. Psalm 51: 1-19 NIV

2. Manning, Brennan. *Abba's Child: the cry of the heart for intimate belonging.* Colorado Springs, CO: NavPress, 1994, 2002, 2005, 50.

3. Manning, *Abba's Child,* 49

4. Ilibagiza, Immaculee. *Left to tell: Discovering God Amidst the Rwandan Holocaust.* Carlsbad, CA: Hay House, 2014.

5. Ilibagiza and Erwin, *Led By Faith,* 192

6. Ilibagiza and Erwin, *Led By Faith,* 192

7. Shore, David, writer. "Nobody's Fault." Season 8, episode,11, In *House MD.* NBC. February 6, 2012.

# Chapter 8
## What's Going On?

1.  Dachel, Anne. *The Autism Cover-up.* New York, NY.: Skyhorse Publishing,2014. P.199
2.  "Vaccine Ingredients and Manufacturer Information." Procon.org, September 19, 2016. https://vaccines.procon.org/view.resource.php?resourceID=005206.
3.  Wells, S.D. "Health Basics: The 11 most toxic vaccine ingredients and their side effects." Natural News. February 29, 2012. https://www.naturalnew.com/035431 vaccine ingredients side p, 4.
4.  Cave, Stephanie, MD. "Injecting Vaccines Before a Child's Blood-Brain Barrier Is Fully Developed." Vaccines: The Outliers. October 8, 2015. https://vaccinesbytheoutliers.wordpress.com/2015/10/08/injecting-vaccines-before-a-child's-blood-brain-barrier-is-fully-developed/.
5.  Habakus, Louise Kuo, M.A., and Mary Holland, J. D. *Vaccine Epidemic.* New York, NY: Skyhorse Publishing,2011,2012. p27-28.
6.  Habakus and Holland, *Vaccine Epidemic,* 28
7.  "CDC estimate 1 in 68 children has been diagnosed with autism spectrum," Center for Disease and Prevention, March 27, 2014. https://www.cdc.gov/media/release/2014/p0327-autism-spectrum-disorder-html.
8.  "Viral Hepatitis," Centers for Disease Control and Prevention, updated May31, 2015, https://www.cdc.gov/hepatitis/hbv/index.htm
9.  NC Hepatitis B Public Health Program Manuel/Vaccination, February 2012, page 4, https://epi.publichealth.nc.gov/cd/lhds/manuels/hepB/docs/hbv_vaccination.pdf
10. "Epidemiology and Prevention of Vaccine-Preventable Diseases-Diphtheria," Centers for Disease Control and Prevention, last revised May 16, 2018 https://www.cdc.gov/vaccines/pubs/pinkbook/dip.html
11. "About Tetanus," Center for Disease Control and Prevention, last reviewed January 10, 2017, https://www.cdc.gov/tetanus/about/index.html
12. "Vaccine Information Statements," Center for Disease Control and Prevention, August 24, 2018, https://www.cdc.gov/vaccines/hcp/vis/vis-statements/dtap.html
13. "Pertussis," Center for Disease Control and Prevention, August 7, 2017, https://www.cdc.gov/pertussis/index.html
14. "Red Alert: The Vaccine Responsible for Half the Awards for Injury and Death," Mercola.com, November 2, 2011, https:/articles.mercola.

com/sites/articles/archives/2011/11/02/why-is-this- vaccine-causing-increased-infant-mortality.aspx

15. Dr Jay Gordon, "The MMR Whistleblower's Article-Opinions about the Results Vary, Draw Your Own Conclusions," drjaygordon.com, January10, 2015, http://drjaygordon.com/vaccinations/the -mmr-whistlebowers-article-opinions-about-the-results-/articles.vary-draw-your-own-conclusion.html

16. Andrew J. Wakefield, "MMR Vaccination and Autism," *The Lancet,* vol. 354, issue 9182, September 11, 1999: 949-950, DOI: https://doi.org/10.1016/S0140-6736(5)75696-8.

17. Habakus and Holland, *Vaccine Epidemic,* 312-314

18. "Timeline: Thimerosal in Vaccines (1999-2010)." Center for Disease Control and Prevention. August 28, 2015, https://www.cdc.gov/vaccinesafety/concerns/thimerosal/timeline.html

19. Bock, Kenneth, Cameron Stauth, and Korri Fink. *Healing the new childhood epidemics: autism, ADHD, asthma, and allergies: the groundbreaking program for the 4-A disorders. New York: Ballantine, 2008.* P. 52

20. "Thimerosal and Vaccines-Thimerosal as a Preservative," FDA U.S. Food and Drug Administration, last updated August 18, 2018. https://www.fda.gov/ForConsumers/ConsumerUpdates/ucm096228.htm#pres.

21. Tracey Watson, "New CDC Study Blows Away Vaccine Propagandists' Claim That Methylmercury is dangerous But Ethylmercury is Safe," naturalnew.com, February21, 2017 https://www.naturalnews.com/2017-02-21-new-cdc-study-blows-away-vaccine-propagandists-claim-that-methylmercury-is-dangerous-but-ethyl-mercury-is-safe.html

22. "Healthcare Wide Hazards-Mercury," OSHA.gov, accessed May 17, 2018, https://www.osha.gov/SLTC/etools/hospital/hazards/mercury/mercury.html

23. Abbott, Marcia Staggs. *A Shocking Discovery: Observations of a Speech/Language Pathologist from1975-2005: What Have We Done to Our Children?* Baltimore. MD: Publish America, 2006. P.44

24. M, Savabieasfahani, M. Hoseing, and S. Goodarzi, "Toxic Metals Are Passed from Mother to Fetus," Nutritionalbalancing.org. 2018, https://nutritionalbalancing.org/center/children/articles/fetus-detox.php.

25. "The Development of the Immunization Schedule," The History of Vaccines.org. January 11, 2018, https://thehistoryofvaccines.org/content/articles/development-immunization-schedule.

26. 09-152 Bruesewitz v. Wyeth, February 22, 2011, Supremecourt.gov, https://www.suprememcourt.gov/opinions/10pdf/09-152.pdf

27. Abbott, Marcia Staggs. *A Shocking Discovery: Observations of a Speech and Language Pathologist from 1975-2005; What Have We Done to Our Children?* Baltimore, MD: Publish America, 2006. P. 44

28. Jim O'Brien, "Mercury Amalgam Toxicity," International Center for Nutritional Research, November 28, 2012, http://www.icnr.com/articles/mercury-amalgam-toxicity.html

29. Bock and Fink, *Healing the new childhood epidemics*, 52

30. Melissa Bailey, "So Long, Hippocrates. Medical Students Choose Their Own Oaths," statnews.com, September 21, 2016, https://www.statnews.com/2016/09/21/hippocratic-oath-medical-students-doctors/

31. "Must-Avoid Foods: Linking GMO to Toxicity and Disease," bodyecology.com, accessed March 4, 2018, https://bodyecology.com/articles/must-avoid-foods-linking-gmo-to-toxicity-and-disease

32. "Joseph Goebbels: On the 'Big Lie'," Jewish Virtual Library-A Project of AICE, 1998-2018 American-Israeli Cooperative Enterprise, https//www.jewishvirtuallibrary.org/about-aice

33. Dachel, *The Autism Cover-up*, 211

34. Staff, TVR "CDC: 1 in 45 Children Diagnosed with Autism" The vaccine Reaction.org. December 8, 2015. https://the vaccinereaction.org/2015/12/cdc-1-in-45-children-diagnosed-with-autism/.

35. Autism Spectrum Disorder, Autism and Developmental Disabilities Monitoring (ADDM) Network, last updated April 26, 2018, https//www.cdc.gov/ncbddd/autism/addm.html

36. Autism Spectrum Disorder, Autism and Developmental Disabilities Monitoring (ADDM) Network, last updated April 26, 2018, https://www.cdc.gov/ncbddd/autism/addm.html

37. Autism Spectrum Disorder, Autism and Developmental Disabilities Monitoring (ADDM) Network, last updated April 26, 2018, https://www.cdc.gov/ncbddd/autism/addm.html

38. "New government survey pegs autism prevalence at 1 in 45," Autism Speaks, November 13, 2015, https://autismspeaks.org/science/science-news/new-government-survey-pegs-autism-prevelance-1-45.

39. Dachel, *The Autism Cover-Up*, 246

40. Silberman, Steve. *NeuroTribes*. Penguin Publishing Group, 2015.

41. Robinson and Aronica, *Creative Schools*, 25

42. Robinson and Aronica, *Creative Schools*, 83.

43. Robinson and Aronica, *Creative Schools*, 101.

44. Freed and Parsons, *Right-Brained Children,* 169

45. Freed and Parsons, *Right-Brained Children, 165*
46. Freed and Parsons, *Right-Brained Children, 169*

## Chapter 9
# The Right Stuff

1. Gottschall, *Breaking the Vicious Cycle*
2. Earaerobics 1997-2004 Cognitive Concepts, Inc.
3. DiCamillo, Kate. *Because of Winn-Dixie.* Somerville, MA: Candlewick Press, 2015
4. Banks, Lynne Reid. *The Indian in the Cupboard.* New York, NY: Random House, 1980
5. Lewis, C.S. *The Lion, the Witch and the Wardrobe.* New York, NY: HarperCollins Publisher 2009.
6. *The War Room,* 2015 film directed by Alex Kendrick through Kenrick Brothers Productions
7. Freed and Parsons, *Right Brained Children, 167*
8. "DSM-IV Diagnostic Classifications," Autistic Disorder (299.00 DSM-IV), Autism-Society.org, accessed January 12, 2018, https//www.autism-society.org/dsm-iv-diagnostic-classifications/

## Chapter 10
# The Potter

1. *The Joy of Painting,* "Mountain Ridge Lake," season 23, episode 3, P.B.S., September 17, 1991.

## Epilogue
1. Manning, *Abba's Child,* 16
2. Manning, Brennan. *Ragamuffin Gospel.* Colorado Springs, Co: Multnomah Books, 1990, 2000, 2005. p 73

## Appendix
1. Conrad, Kendall and Elaine Gottschall, *Eat Well, Feel Well. More Than 150 Delicious Specific Carbohydrate-Diet Compliant Recipes.* New York: Three Rivers Press, 2010. p 27

# About the Author

Anna Gideon is a registered nurse with vast experience in both critical care and the emergency room. She is also an accomplished pianist and currently teaches piano in Highlands Ranch, Colorado, where she lives with her three teenagers, her husband, and her dog Mabel.

Gideon is a member of Cherry Hills Community Church as well as Moms in Prayer International. This is her first published book.

Please visit Anna's website at annagideon.com.

CPSIA information can be obtained
at www.ICGtesting.com
Printed in the USA
BVHW031447180419
545922BV00001B/23/P

9 781973 646587